AMAZING ASIA

WRITTEN BY
RASHMI SIRDESHPANDE

ILLUSTRATED BY
JASON LYON

WIDE EYED EDITIONS

CONTENTS

WELCOME TO ASIA / 4

WELCOME TO ASIA

In this book, we will dive deep into this vast and epic continent,

looking at its incredible past, its fascinating present, and its exciting future.

We will explore five geographic regions:

East Asia, Southeast Asia, South Asia, North and Central Asia and West Asia.

Within these pages we're going to

— go back in time to understand each region's history

— get to know each region's people and cultures

— navigate stunning landscapes and encounter incredible wildlife

— explore the most spectacular sights

— meet some amazing change-makers

— and see what the future may hold for Asia's regions and for the continent as a whole.

Finally, we'll look at GLOBAL ASIA — from the history of Asian migration to pockets of

Asian culture all over the planet and the many ways in which Asia has influenced the world.

Enjoy your journey into this beautiful continent. Happy reading!

- -

MAPS

The maps in this book aren't atlas maps. They are not drawn to scale and the icons within them are there to give you a flavour of what you might encounter in each region. The main purpose of these maps is to introduce you to the various parts of Asia and the wonderfully diverse countries you will discover in this continent. You may find that other resources divide Asian countries into these five regions slightly differently from how we've done it in this book, but we're covering the same ground. You will also learn that some of the borders between these countries are disputed — we'll look at some instances of this, but it is sadly inevitable because borders are drawn up by humans, often as a result of politics, conflict, and the building and breaking of empires, so they don't take into account the needs of the people or ensure a fair division of resources.

DATES

When you go back far enough in history, timelines are tricky. Historians are still debating many of the dates featured in this book. We have included commonly accepted dates and ranges, but new discoveries are made all the time that can completely transform our understanding of an era.

Kabuki dance

WHAT IS ASIA?

Asia is the largest continent, covering around a third of all the land on our planet and accounting for two-thirds of the world's population — that's over 4.7 billion people (2.8 billion between just China and India). A continent of contrasts, it has a stunning array of landscapes and wildlife, and a vibrant mix of cultures and religions.

Bengal tiger

Vaadhoo Island, the Maldives

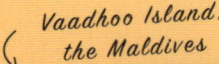

Yi Peng Lantern Festival

Floating market

Ishtar Gate, ancient Babylon

Akhal-Teke horse

LANDSCAPES

In Asia, you will find the very highest point on the planet (Mount Everest) as well as the very lowest on land (the Dead Sea). The landscapes here are incredibly diverse, and include vast deserts and steppes, lush rainforests, rugged mountains, mighty rivers, crystal lakes, karst islands and lava caves.

WILDLIFE

This continent is rich in wildlife. It is home to the beautiful blue and green peafowl, and to rare and endangered animals such as Sunda pangolins, giant pandas, Bengal tigers, Asian elephants and orangutans. Its waters are filled with fascinating marine life from Irrawaddy dolphins and dugongs to whale sharks, hawksbill turtles and coral reefs.

CULTURE

As is the case with every continent, Asia is a melting pot of diverse cultures. The region has a long and rich history of storytelling, reflected in its folklore, legends, poetic traditions and dance dramas. Countless forms of dance and music have developed across the continent as its people have come together along the Silk Roads or through the expansion of empires. Today, contemporary music from the region often includes echoes of these classical roots.

RELIGION

Asia is the birthplace of many world religions and belief systems, including the Bahá'í faith, Buddhism, Christianity, Confucianism, Islam, Jainism, Judaism, Hinduism, Shintō, Sikhi, Taoism and Zoroastrianism! They have all inspired amazing instances of art, music, poetry and architecture.

LIFESTYLES

What do you think of when you think of life in Asia? Soaring city skylines and busy urban streets? Or a rural paradise where "the old ways" are still treasured and ancient traditions are kept alive? Asia is all these things and many, many more in between. From its indigenous groups with their deep connection to the natural world to the residents of quiet villages and fast-paced towns and cities, lifestyles vary – a beautiful blend of the old and the new.

ARCHITECTURE

Asia is home to some incredible works of architecture – from its elaborately designed and decorated temples, pagodas, mosques, mausoleums and other monuments to its exquisite forts, palaces and gardens. Contemporary pieces are a marvel too, with bold modern designs and skyscrapers that stretch up to the skies (the top five world's tallest buildings are in Asia!).

Qawwali music

Abida Parveen

THE CONTINENT OF ASIA

This incredible continent stretches all the way from the Arctic Circle in the north to the equator in the south, and is bounded by the Mediterranean and Black seas in the west and the Pacific Ocean in the east. Here you will discover everything from dry deserts to lush rainforests, vast steppes to magnificent mountains, and ancient villages and cities to sprawling modern metropolises.

The DEAD SEA in West Asia is the lowest point on land on the surface of the Earth.

NORTH AND CENTRAL ASIA

EAST ASIA

SOUTH ASIA

WEST ASIA

Asia is home to some rare and WONDROUS ANIMALS – from giant pandas, Bengal tigers and Asian elephants to orangutans, king cobras and Komodo dragons.

Of the **WORLD'S HIGHEST MOUNTAINS** (all over 8,000 metres above sea level), 14 can be found in the Himalayan and Karakoram mountain ranges of Asia, including Mount Everest (Sāgarmāthā in Nepali and Chomolungma in Tibetan), the highest peak above sea level on the planet.

Some of the world's largest **MEGACITIES** (metropolises with a population of over 10 million people) can be found in Asia, including Tokyo, Delhi, Shanghai and Dhaka.

SOUTHEAST ASIA

Asia is the birthplace of some of the **EARLIEST CIVILISATIONS** in the world's recorded history, including Ancient Sumer, the Indus Valley Civilisation and the Shang dynasty.

Over 2,300 **LANGUAGES** are spoken in Asia. More than 700 are spoken in Indonesia alone.

FASCINATING FACTS

WEST ASIA

Yerevan, the capital of **ARMENIA**, is one of the world's oldest continuously inhabited cities – 29 years older than Rome!

In the winter, pelicans and flamingos flock to the lakes and wetlands along the Caspian Sea in the East of **AZERBAIJAN**.

In the Bronze Age, **BAHRAIN** was Dilmun (or Telmun), the centre of an important trading empire, connecting Mesopotamia with the Indus Valley civilisation.

CYPRUS is famous for its hellim (or halloumi), a squeaky, chewy, high-protein cheese invented there during the Byzantine era.

The people of **GEORGIA** call their country Sakartvelo.

IRAN is the last wild home to the critically endangered Asiatic cheetah or Persian cheetah, which used to roam from West Asia to the Indian subcontinent.

The 3,500-year-old epic poem the Epic of Gilgamesh was found in the Library of Ashurbanipal in **IRAQ**, written on a clay tablet in cuneiform script.

In Tel Aviv in **ISRAEL**, you will find juice stands filled with brightly coloured fruits at what feels like every corner.

The national flower of **JORDAN** is the rare and beautiful black iris, which blooms across the country in the spring.

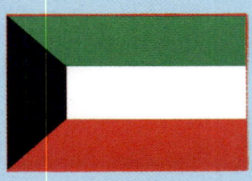
Bordered by Saudi Arabia and Iraq, **KUWAIT** was the very first country in the Gulf to establish its own parliament.

The mountains of **LEBANON** were once covered in cedar trees. Lebanese cedar was also used by the Phoenicians, who were great ancient mariners, to build their boats.

All over **OMAN** you will find elaborate double-sided wooden doors in all kinds of colours and decorated with beautiful patterns and motifs.

The traditional Levantine folk dance dabke is very popular in **PALESTINE** and an important part of Palestinian culture and identity.

QATAR is the flattest country in the world after the Maldives and is mostly made up of low-lying desert.

Ardah is the national dance of **SAUDI ARABIA**. It is a traditional Bedouin sword dance set against the backdrop of mesmerising drums and poetic chants.

Damascus, the capital of **SYRIA**, is also known as Madinat-al-Yasmin ("City of Jasmine") because of the delicately fragranced jasmine flowers that climb the walls, arches and buildings.

Istanbul in **TÜRKIYE** is a transcontinental city, with its Asian and European sides separated by the shimmering Bosphorus Strait.

The **UNITED ARAB EMIRATES** (UAE) is a federation of seven emirates, each with their own ruling families and identities. Abu Dhabi is the largest emirate.

The silversmiths of **YEMEN** were once renowned across the Arab world for their jewellery and their hilts and sheaths for swords and daggers.

SOUTH ASIA

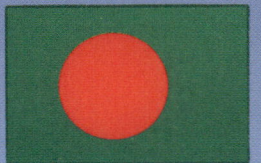

Armenia, Azerbaijan, Cyprus, Georgia, Kazakhstan, Russia and Türkiye are transcontinental countries. They are part of Asia but some of their territory lies in Europe.

SOUTHEAST ASIA

Over 70% of **BRUNEI** is covered in lush green tropical rainforests.

CAMBODIA is home to rare and endangered animals such as the Asian elephant, the giant softshell turtle and the Irrawaddy dolphin.

With 130 active volcanoes, **INDONESIA** is a hot spot in the Ring of Fire, a highly volatile region of seismic activity in the Pacific Ocean.

The Plain of Jars in **LAOS** is a mysterious plateau with thousands of huge stone jars, some of which might be over 3,000 years old. No one knows why they are there or what they were used for!

Durian fruit is grown in **MALAYSIA**. People either love it or hate it but its smell is so strong that it is banned in many public places such as hotels!

In **MYANMAR**, the Intha fishermen of Inle Lake row with one leg, as doing so gives them a clearer view over the water reeds and keeps their hands free to manage their cone-shaped fishing nets.

SINGAPORE is famous for its Singaporean-English (Singlish!). A number of Singlish words have made it into the Oxford English Dictionary, including the iconic "lah", which is often used for emphasis.

The tropical rainforest in Khao Sok National Park in **THAILAND** is believed to be 160 million years old, making it one of the oldest rainforests in the world and much older than the Amazon!

The **PHILIPPINES** is made up of more than 7,600 islands but only around 2,000 are inhabited.

TIMOR-LESTE is Asia's newest country. It became an independent nation in 2002.

Water puppetry in **VIETNAM** is a tradition dating back to the 11th century in the villages of the Red River Delta.

AFGHANISTAN is famous for its sweet fruits, including pomegranates, melons, grapes and apricots.

At 120 kilometres in length, Cox's Bazar in **BANGLADESH** is the longest unbroken natural sea beach on the planet.

BHUTAN is known in the local language Dzongkha as Druk Yul ("Land of the Thunder Dragon").

With a population of over 1.4 billion people (and growing!), **INDIA** is the most populous country in the world.

The sparkling turquoise waters of the **MALDIVES** are home to all kinds of sea life from manta rays and whale sharks to five out of seven species of turtle.

Lumbini, a Buddhist pilgrimage site in the Terai plains of **NEPAL**, is the birthplace of Prince Siddhartha Gautama, who became Lord Buddha and the founder of Buddhism.

K2, the highest mountain in **PAKISTAN**, is the second highest mountain in the world and considered one of the deadliest to climb.

SRI LANKA is known for its fragrant Ceylon tea, which is considered to be one of the finest teas in the world.

EAST ASIA

Officially known as the People's Republic of China, **CHINA** is a vast country, occupying much of East Asia. But even though it is almost as wide as the US, it only has one official time zone – Beijing time. The US has six!

Shinkansen (bullet trains) in **JAPAN** are incredibly fast (they often run at speeds of over 300km/hr) and astonishingly punctual (often to the second!).

The Khongoryn Els sand dunes in the Gobi Desert of **MONGOLIA** are known as "the Singing Dunes" because of the sound that is made when the winds move the sand.

Mountains and hills make up 80% of **NORTH KOREA**'s landscape.

Like its neighbour, **SOUTH KOREA** is largely mountainous. It is made up of around 3,400 islands, including the beautiful volcanic Jeju Island with its extensive lava caves.

Between North Korea and South Korea there is a buffer zone called the Demilitarised Zone (the DMZ)

NORTH AND CENTRAL ASIA

KAZAKHSTAN means "Land of the Wanderers", a name that draws on the nation's nomadic culture.

KYRGYZSTAN is home to mountains, canyons, glaciers, lakes and the world's largest natural walnut forest.

RUSSIA stretches over Europe and Asia. The regions of **Siberia** and the **Russian Far East** fall within Asia.

Thanks to its glaciers and its network of rivers, almost all of the power generated in **TAJIKISTAN** is hydropower.

The ancient site of Merv in **TURKMENISTAN** is the remains of a 4,000-year-old city on the Silk Road.

The Muruntau gold mine in the Kyzylkum Desert of **UZBEKISTAN** is one of the largest in the world.

ANCIENT EMPIRES

In this book, you will discover some of the incredible ancient empires of Asia. Here are just a few snapshots of the mighty military and maritime powers and stunning cities that we'll explore.

Phoenician ship

WEST ASIA

It is here, in ancient Mesopotamia, that the Sumerians invented one of the world's first writing systems – CUNEIFORM. It is also here, in the Levant, that the skilled seafarers, the Phoenicians, built innovative ships using wood from the famed cedars of Lebanon. And it is in this region that the world saw the rise of the extensive Achaemenid Empire (the Persian Empire), with its beautiful capital at PARSA (PERSEPOLIS), as well as the powerful Ottoman Empire, which took on the Byzantine Empire (the eastern half of the Roman Empire) and captured Constantinople (now Istanbul in Türkiye).

Parsa (Persepolis)

Cuneiform tablet

Taj Mahal

SOUTH ASIA

Vijayanagar Empire architecture

The ancient and expansive Indus Valley Civilisation flourished here, with its well-planned cities and carefully constructed water and drainage systems. So did the Chola Empire, a maritime power that greatly influenced Southeast Asia. Many magnificent empires took shape in South Asia, including the Gupta Empire with its contributions to science and literature, the Vijayanagar Empire with its elaborate temples and palaces, and the Mughal Empire with its incredible architecture, art and music.

NORTH AND CENTRAL ASIA

This was the stomping ground of the SCYTHIAN TRIBES, fierce nomadic warriors who fought on horseback. The first Turkic empire formed here – the Göktürk Empire – long before the rise of the Ottoman Empire. Central Asia was also the home of the Chagatai Khanate, led by the second son of Genghis Khan, and the powerful Timurid Empire, the last great empire to rise from the Central Asian Steppes.

Amaterasu

EAST ASIA

The Shang dynasty originated here in the Yellow River basin in ancient China. It was the first Chinese dynasty in written records and famous for its writing system and its bronze weapons and vessels. East Asia was also home to the three rival kingdoms of ancient Korea, the Yamato clan of Japan (who claimed to be descendants of the sun goddess, AMATERASU), the brave samurai warriors of the Edo period, and the mighty Mongol Empire led by Genghis Khan (Chinggis Khan in Mongolian).

Kingdom of Ayutthaya

SOUTHEAST ASIA

The Srivijaya Kingdom, based on the island of Sumatra, was famed for its legendary riches. The Khmer Empire of Cambodia also rose to power here, bringing with it all kinds of impressive construction projects from roads, canals and temple-hospitals to the vast ANGKOR WAT. Later, the Siamese (Thai) KINGDOM OF AYUTTHAYA flourished in this region, building its capital into a wealthy cosmopolitan trading hub.

Angkor Wat

THE SILK ROADS

No book about Asia would be complete without a look into the magnificent world of the Silk Roads. These were vast networks of routes connecting China with West Asia and Europe, enabling the flow of people, goods and ideas between the East and West for around 1,500 years up to the mid-15th century. These routes were studded with spectacular cities as well as caravanserais – roadside inns where travelling merchants found shelter and exchanged merchandise, stories, languages and culture.

Here are just some of the many cities that grew and flourished over time on the Silk Roads, becoming incredible cosmopolitan hubs:

THE FLOW OF GOODS

Many goods were traded on the Silk Roads, including silk, tea, spices, medicines, fruits and nuts, ceramics, precious stones and metals, and even horses! Merchants often travelled in caravans – groups of merchants, pilgrims, hired guards and other travellers, journeying together to protect against bandits, especially when crossing deserts and steppes. People rarely travelled all the way from east to west or west to east with their wares – instead, trade (and ideas) flowed through a series of merchants along the Silk Roads.

THE FLOW OF IDEAS

Inventions such as paper, printing and gunpowder spread from China through the rest of Asia and into Europe. Art, science and languages spread in all directions in much the same way as merchants, scholars, diplomats and other travellers moved along the Silk Roads. So did religions such as Buddhism, Zoroastrianism, Judaism, Christianity and, later, Islam. As ideas were exchanged and discussed, they blended and transformed along these roads, shaping local beliefs, culture and architecture.

THE DARK SIDE OF THE SILK ROADS

Today, we consider freedom to be a basic human right but many hundreds of thousands of people were enslaved (often by raiding armies) and traded along these routes as property to be bought and sold. The Vikings of Scandinavia, in particular, made a lot of profit in West and Central Asia from this terrible trade, which was tragically widespread across the length of the Silk Roads, from Ireland to China. War and conflict also made their way along the Silk Roads as did disease, including the Black Death — the bubonic plague that killed as many as 200 million people across Asia and Europe in the 14th century.

Zheng He

MARITIME TRADING ROUTES

The maritime Silk Roads were networks of sea routes connecting cities across Asia. But maritime trading routes in Asia go back many thousands of years to trade links between ancient Mesopotamia and the Indus Valley Civilisation. Even the more "modern" routes navigated by the famed Ming dynasty admiral Zheng He over 600 years ago were established long before the arrival of the first European colonial vessels. These routes and Zheng He's voyages helped to spread Chinese culture, crafts and innovations, and built strong trade links that stretched from East Asia, Southeast Asia and India as far as the Arabian peninsula and the coast of East Africa.

EAST ASIA

East Asia, like the rest of this epic continent, is a place of contrasts. Today, the remnants of the region's ancient empires sit alongside its striking landscapes, and the bustling cities filled with skyscrapers and shopping malls are hotbeds of innovation.

The takhi horses of **MONGOLIA**, which are also known as Przewalski's horses, are an important national symbol for Mongolians.

CHINA (officially known as the People's Republic of China) is the source of many world-changing inventions, including paper, printing, the compass, silk, and even ice cream in its early form – a mixture of milk and rice, frozen in snow.

MONGOLIA

CHINA

The **Yangtze River** in China is the longest river in Asia and the third longest in the world, after the Amazon and the Nile. Teeming with wildlife, the Yangtze flows for 6,300 km from the glacial meltwaters of the Tanggula Mountains to the city of Shanghai and the East China Sea.

Tibet

ASIA

Tibet is an autonomous region of China. It has its own local government and can make its own laws.

THE RING OF FIRE

Located in the volatile Ring of Fire, which stretches across parts of Asia and the Pacific basin, Japan and Taiwan are frequently hit by earthquakes and tremors. Some of these have been catastrophic, but thankfully most are minor.

Known as the "hermit kingdom", **NORTH KOREA** is an extremely secretive nation. It maintains strict control over its citizens, including controlling their TV and radio stations, internet and music.

The land between North Korea and South Korea is called the **DMZ** (the Demilitarised Zone), a buffer zone established to maintain peace between these two nations.

Seoul, the capital of **SOUTH KOREA**, sits on the Han River and is a bustling megacity, famous for its technology, its street food, and for being the home of K-pop music and K-dramas.

JAPAN is an "archipelago" – a string of islands, sweeping across the western Pacific Ocean. The mix of warm- and cold-water currents makes it the perfect spot for marine life to thrive – from bottlenose dolphins to hammerhead sharks and sea turtles.

NORTH KOREA

SOUTH KOREA

JAPAN

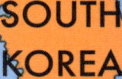

Officially called The Republic of China, **Taiwan** sees itself as an independent nation, but China considers Taiwan a part of its territory.

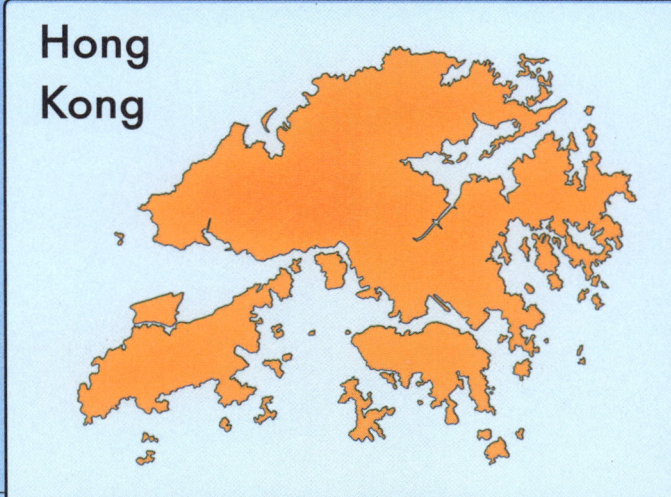

Hong Kong

Taiwan

Hong Kong

Macao

Taiwan has over 100 natural hot springs, with mineral-rich waters bubbling up from the depths of the Earth. It also has cold springs, mud springs and sea-floor hot springs.

Hong Kong and **Macao** are special administrative regions of China. This means they have their own currencies, and their own legal systems and governments, but they are still considered part of China. In 2020, the Chinese government cracked down on protests in Hong Kong with strict laws limiting freedom of speech. Many activists, journalists and lawmakers have been silenced and arrested under these laws and this has been a growing source of tension between Hong Kong and mainland China.

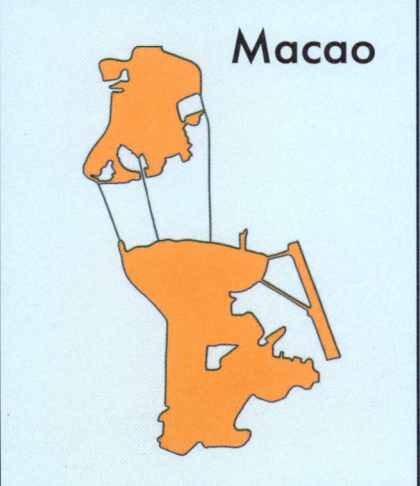

Macao

A JOURNEY THROUGH TIME

The birthplace of powerful civilisations such as Imperial China, ancient Japan, the kingdoms of Korea and the Mongol Empire, East Asia is rich in history. Here, as in other parts of Asia, great dynasties have risen and fallen. In recent years, too, wars and politics have shaped the region.

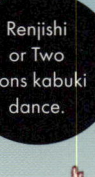

1600–1046 BCE
THE SHANG DYNASTY

This was the first dynasty in China's recorded history. The Shang were skilled in BRONZE-WORK and created bronze swords and spearheads, which, along with chariots, gave them an advantage over enemies in battle. They also developed the first form of Chinese writing, and wrote questions to the gods on ORACLE BONES made of animal bones and turtle shells.

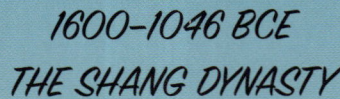

221–c.207 BCE
THE QIN DYNASTY

The name "China" may well come from the Qin dynasty, a short-lived dynasty that unified the warring states of China and built the first Chinese empire. Qin Shi Huang was a ruthless military leader. It is said that he burned books that didn't support his thinking and had 460 Confucian scholars executed. When he died, he was buried with an army of over 8,000 life-size TERRACOTTA WARRIORS to guard him in death.

Renjishi or Two Lions kabuki dance.

1603–c.1867 CE
THE EDO PERIOD IN JAPAN

This was the era of the Tokugawa shogunate, a military dictatorship led by the Tokugawa family. It was a time of strict controls, peace and stability, and a time when Japan closed its doors to most of the outside world. Arts and culture flourished, and the Edo period saw the development of KABUKI THEATRE, professional sumo wrestling, woodblock printing and new forms of poetry and painting.

Kublai Khan

훈민정음

한글

The Korean script HANGEUL was developed under King Sejong the Great.

1392–1910 CE
THE JOSEON DYNASTY IN KOREA

Founded by King Taejo, the Joseon Dynasty was the last imperial dynasty of Korea. It was considered a golden age of art, culture and creativity in Korea. It reached its peak under Taejo's grandson, King Sejong the Great, who was a patron of the arts and science, and oversaw a period of great innovation and invention.

1911 AND 1966 CE
THE CHINESE REVOLUTION AND THE CULTURAL REVOLUTION

The Chinese Revolution established the Republic of China, ending around 2,000 years of imperial rule. Things changed rapidly over the years as an authoritarian form of communism took root. In 1966, CHAIRMAN MAO ZEDONG rolled out the Cultural Revolution, violently cracking down on critics and "old ideas", and plunging the country into chaos. The revolution was called to an end in 1976 but historians estimate that between 500,000 and 2 million people lost their lives during this period.

57 BCE–668 CE
THE THREE KINGDOMS PERIOD

During this period, the Korean peninsula was ruled by three rival kingdoms: Goguryeo, the largest and a mighty military force; Baekje, an agricultural, maritime society; and Silla, a small kingdom with an elite group of warriors called the HWARANG (Flowering Youth). Alliances shifted and the fighting was bitter but Silla eventually won, establishing a unified Korea.

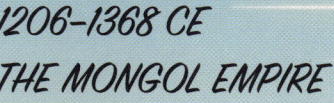

1206–1368 CE
THE MONGOL EMPIRE

Genghis Khan (known as Chinggis Khan in Mongolia) united the nomadic groups of Mongolia and led a brutal campaign to create the largest contiguous land empire in history, covering 23 million square kilometres! In 1279, his grandson, KUBLAI KHAN, went on to conquer China and establish the Yuan Dynasty.

250–710 CE
THE YAMATO CLAN IN JAPAN

This imperial family claimed to be descendants of AMATERASU, the sun goddess. As the ruler of the heavens, she was one of the most important figures in the Shintō tradition. The emperor headed the imperial court but the real power lay with clan leaders from influential noble families.

1945 CE
HIROSHIMA AND NAGASAKI

In August 1945, during the Second World War, United States (US) air forces dropped an atomic bomb on the Japanese cities of Hiroshima and Nagasaki. It was the first time a nuclear weapon had ever been deployed in war and the devastation was immense. The cities were reduced to rubble and it is believed that over 200,000 people were killed. By mid-August, Japan surrendered, but what was done could not be undone.

The Genbaku Dome: Hiroshima Peace Memorial

1950–1953 CE
THE KOREAN WAR

At the end of the Second World War, North Korea was occupied by Soviet Russia and South Korea was occupied by US troops. Both outside forces withdrew by 1949 but the border between north and south was heavily disputed. War broke out in 1950 when North Korea invaded South Korea. A US-led United Nations army stepped in to support South Korea, while the Soviet Union and China supported North Korea. It was a battle of ideology – capitalism against communism. Eventually, a deal was struck to create a 4-km-wide demilitarised zone (the DMZ) between the two nations as a buffer to keep the peace.

HISTORY SPOTLIGHTS

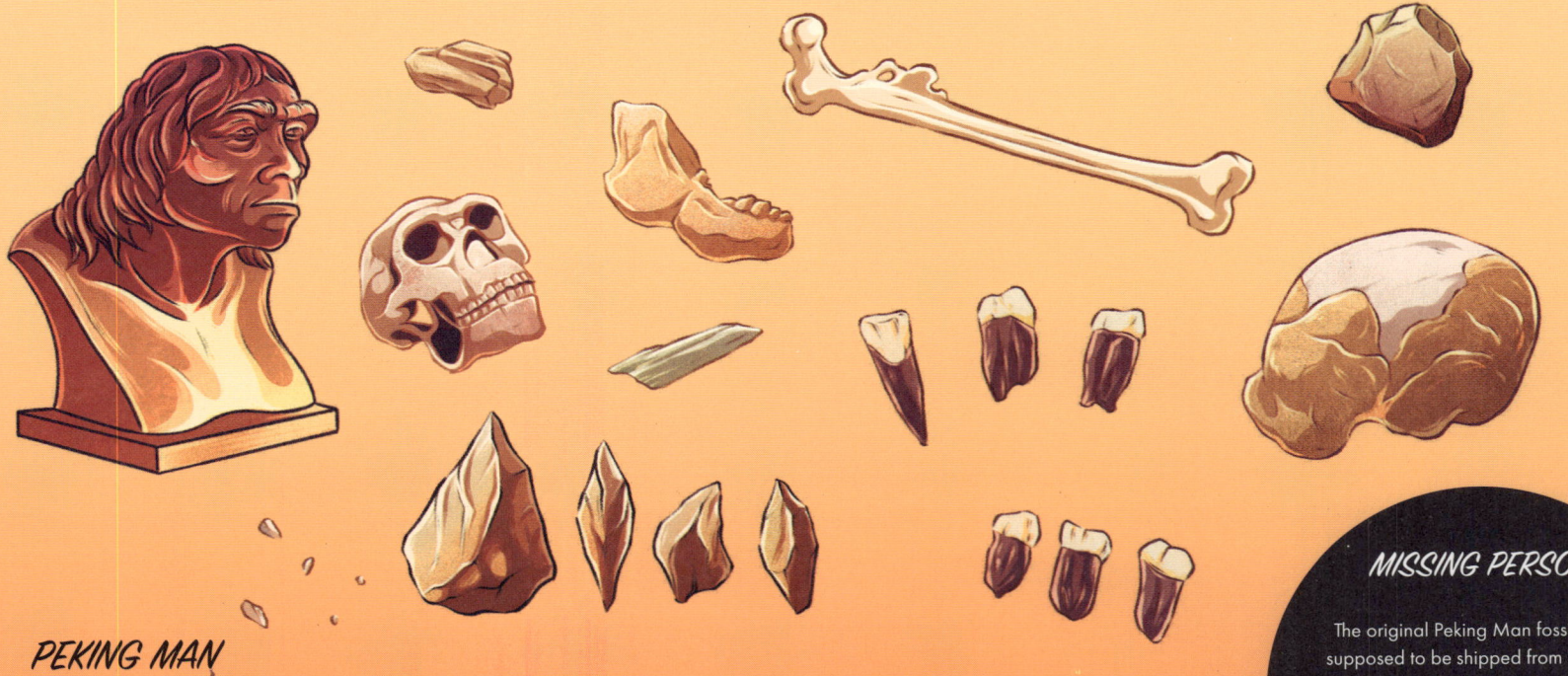

PEKING MAN

In the 1920s and 1930s, around 200 fossils from 40–50 individuals were discovered in the caves of Zhoukoudian outside Beijing, China. These skulls, teeth and other bones came to be known as Peking Man. They are thought to be up to 780,000 years old and belong to a species called *Homo erectus*, an early hominin related to humans (*Homo sapiens*). *Homo erectus* was the first of our ancient relatives to have human-like proportions, the first to migrate out of Africa, where all early human life began, and may even have been the first to control and use fire.

MISSING PERSON

The original Peking Man fossils were supposed to be shipped from China to the US during the Second World War but disappeared and never made it. Luckily, casts were made but no one quite knows what happened to the originals so they can't be studied and many questions about Peking Man remain unanswered.

GENGHIS KHAN

Genghis Khan was born around 1162 on the Mongolian steppe, and he was originally called Temüjin. When Temüjin was just nine, his father was murdered and his mother and her seven children were thrown out of their tribe and had to fend for themselves, hunting and foraging for survival. Temüjin was enslaved by rival clans in his teens but managed to escape and grew into a powerful and feared leader, uniting the nomadic Mongol tribes in 1206 and taking the name Chinggis Khan (Genghis Khan in the West).

Genghis Khan is known for his ruthless campaigns to expand his empire. Historians think 40 million lives were lost during his conquests. But there was a lesser-known side to him too – he outlawed the kidnapping and selling of Mongol women, he banned torture and the enslavement of Mongols, and he allowed freedom of religion.

Weapons used by the samurai evolved over time but the most famous is the KATANA, a razor-sharp sword with a curved blade.

THE SAMURAI
("THOSE WHO SERVE")

The samurai were bold warriors who dominated Japan from the 12th to the 19th centuries. They rose to power initially because of their skills in horse-riding, archery and sword-fighting but later came to value the literary arts as well as martial arts – many samurai were poets who could wield both the pen and the sword. They wore heavy, finely crafted armour with increasingly elaborate designs and trained in weaponry and spirituality from a young age.

While there are instances of great betrayals and brutality, the samurai warrior code, bushido (the way of the warrior), was based around the concept of honour, integrity and loyalty to their lords, the daimyo. Samurai were also expected to show incredible self-control as well as courage in the face of death.

SEJONG THE GREAT

King Sejong the Great ruled between 1418 and 1450, a period which is considered a golden age in Korea, and he was seen as one of the greatest Korean kings. He was a big believer in education and is best known for developing Hangeul, a simple and elegant Korean writing system. It was much easier to learn than the Chinese writing system, which took years to master. At a time when most of the population was illiterate, this was a hugely important innovation. At first, the new script was met with a lot of resistance but it meant a big leap in the country's literacy and, over time, it became a great source of national pride.

1989 TIANANMEN SQUARE PROTESTS

On 4th May, 1989, following weeks of smaller protests, tens of thousands of peaceful pro-democracy student protesters marched through Beijing to Tiananmen Square calling for changes to how the country was run. By 19th May, a million supporters had joined them. On 4th June, the Chinese authorities brought in military troops and tanks to crush the protests. They opened fire on protesters, killing at least 10,000 people and wounding many more. This devastating event sent shockwaves throughout the world.

PEOPLE AND CULTURE

THE HAN PEOPLE

Of the 56 state-recognised ethnic groups in China, the Han are by far the largest, making up over 90% of the population of mainland China (that's over 1.2 billion people!). The Han speak seven Chinese dialects and Mandarin is the most common. Their name is derived from the Han dynasty, which ruled China from 206 BCE to 220 CE, a period of great innovation. Today, Han people are found all over China and in many parts of Southeast Asia as well as the wider world. In fact, they're the largest ethnic group on the planet.

THE RYUKYUAN PEOPLE

Numbering around 1.4 million, the Ryukyuan people of Japan are the indigenous inhabitants of the Ryukyu Islands, which form an arc from the Japanese island of Kyushu all the way to Taiwan. Once an independent kingdom and a stopping point for traders between Japan, China, Korea and Southeast Asia, these islands have developed their own unique cultures with a mix of influences.

Traditional Ryukyuan pottery, YACHIMUN in the local dialect, is a centuries-old art form. It blends elements from Chinese, Korean and Japanese ceramics.

CALLIGRAPHY

Calligraphy, the art of writing with beautiful brush strokes, has long been honoured in China, Korea and Japan. Known as shufa in Chinese and shodō in Japanese, in Korean it is called seoye and it takes years to master. Every scholar is said to need "four friends" (munbangsawoo in Korean): mulberry paper, a brush, an ink stick and an ink stone.

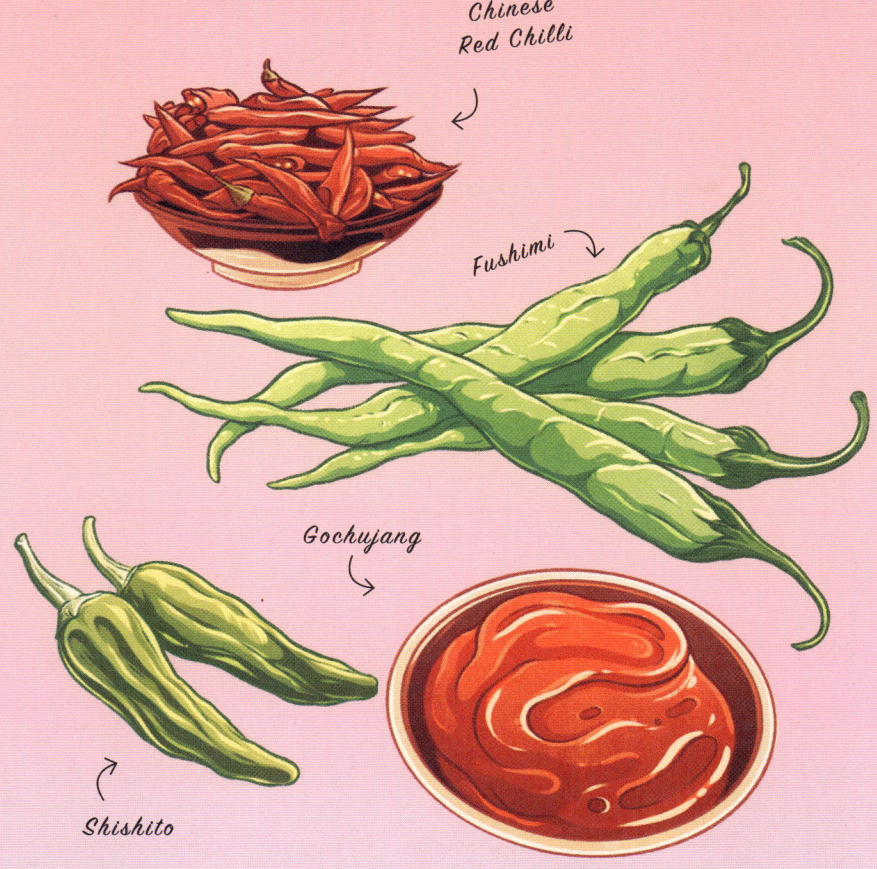

Chinese
Red Chilli

Fushimi

Gochujang

Shishito

RED HOT CHILLIES

Chillies are native to South America but they are loved in many parts of East Asia, especially in places like Sichuan and Hunan in China, where locals like their food with a fiery heat! In Hunan, there is even an annual chilli pepper festival with daily chilli-eating contests! Milder chillies have their place in East Asian cuisine too, such as the Fushimi and Shishito chillies from Japan. Korean gochujang, for example, is a popular red chilli paste with a mix of savoury, sweet and spicy notes and, while some versions are extremely hot, others are milder.

KINTSUGI means to join with gold and is the 15th-century Japanese art of repairing broken pottery with tree-sap lacquer and liquid or powdered precious metals. It celebrates the object's history instead of hiding it and makes it even more beautiful, teaching us to accept imperfections and mistakes.

CHADŌ: THE WAY OF TEA

Originating in China, tea houses and tea ceremonies are found across East Asia with regional variations. The Japanese tea ceremony (or CHADŌ, the way of tea) is rooted in Zen Buddhism and is the skilful art of preparing, serving and drinking matcha, a powdered green tea. It is based on four key principles set out by 16th-century tea master Sen no Rikyū: wa (harmony), kei (respect), sei (purity) and jaku (tranquillity). For both the host and the guests, it is a break from the busy world and a chance to slow down, pay attention to and appreciate the little things, and find inner peace.

THE KHALKHA

The Khalkha make up over 80% of the people of Mongolia. Historically, they were a nomadic people who moved four or five times a year to find fresh pastures for their herds. Today, more than half the population lives in urban areas but many still live in dome-shaped, movable tents called GERS.

Gers are furnished with a central fireplace, beds, chairs, stools, wooden floors and brightly coloured fabrics. They might also have TVs and radios and some have solar panels too! The wooden doors are often painted in bright orange and blue and are always south-facing, making the most of the sunlight and protecting against the northern and north-westerly winds.

WILDLIFE AND LANDSCAPES

East Asia has a dazzling array of stunning landscapes. Here you will find everything from scorching deserts and volcanic islands to mountains, forests and coastal wetlands. These richly diverse habitats are home to a wide range of flora and fauna.

MIGRATORY BIRDS

Twice a year, 50 million migratory birds travel along the East Asian–Australasian Flyway, an avian route from Alaska and Russia to Australia and New Zealand. Many thousands of them, including cranes and shorebirds, stop to refuel at the mudflats of North Korea's Yellow Sea and the marshlands of the DMZ (Demilitarised Zone) between North and South Korea. For the BAR-TAILED GODWIT, this is the only stop on its long journey across the planet.

JAPANESE MACAQUES

Japanese macaques have long, thick hair and distinctive red faces and can be found on three of the four main islands of Japan in a range of forest and mountain habitats. In Jigokudani Monkey Park, during the winter, these "snow monkeys" can often be seen huddled together or bathing in hot springs for warmth.

BAYANZAG – THE "FLAMING CLIFFS" OF MONGOLIA

Located deep in the Gobi Desert, the blazing red cliffs and canyons of Bayanzag – the "Flaming Cliffs" – make up one of the world's most famous palaeontological sites. This is where fossilised dinosaur eggs were first discovered. Other finds include the 80-million-year-old fossils of the fierce Velociraptor, star of the Jurassic Park movies, and the Protoceratops, a small relative of the Triceratops.

THE FLOATING MOUNTAINS OF CHINA

With its breath-taking quartz-sandstone pillars and dense emerald forests, ZHANGJIAJIE NATIONAL FOREST PARK in the Hunan Province of China was the inspiration behind the mountains of Pandora in the blockbuster movie *Avatar*. They are known as "floating mountains" because when the mist and clouds gather, the pillars appear to be suspended in the sky.

THE LAVA TUBES OF JEJU ISLAND

The underground flow of magma from volcanic eruptions on Jeju Island in South Korea has created an extensive system of lava caves or tubes. The tubes are dark and cool with colourful carbonate roofs and floors.

GIANT PANDAS

Once found throughout southern and eastern China, giant pandas now live in thick bamboo forests in the misty mountains of southwest and central China. Their diet consists almost entirely of bamboo shoots and leaves, which they munch on for around 12–14 hours a day. They don't even stop eating to hibernate! Thanks to conservation efforts, these iconic and much-loved bears are no longer endangered, but they are still vulnerable with only around 1,860 left in the wild.

SPECTACULAR SIGHTS

From palaces, temples and soaring skyscrapers
to stunning landscapes, East Asia has an abundance of historical and
cultural landmarks and natural wonders.

MOUNT FUJI

Rising to the sky with a beautiful symmetry, Mount Fuji is surrounded by the Fuji Five Lakes and a number of Shintō shrines. It is the spiritual symbol of Japan and a source of inspiration for many artists and poets. The Japanese word goraiko means "the arrival of light" and captures the joy and gratitude experienced when watching a sunrise from Mount Fuji's summit.

Made up of three layers of volcanos and sitting on the junction of three tectonic plates, Mount Fuji is an active volcano. It last erupted in 1707, a time when samurai warriors still roamed the land and trained at the foot of the mountain.

THE GREAT WALL OF CHINA

Winding through mountains, grasslands and deserts like the body of a dragon, the Great Wall stretches over 20,000 km (with about a quarter made up of natural boundaries, such as rivers). That's half the circumference of the Earth! Work began under the Qin dynasty around 220 BCE and took over 2,000 years with different dynasties adding their own walls, fortresses, beacon towers and barracks.

TAIPEI 101

Taipei 101, a skyscraper in Taiwan, was once the tallest building on the planet. Influenced by bamboo stalks and traditional pagodas, it is made up of eight sections. Eight is a lucky number in Chinese culture, representing wealth and good fortune.

GYEONGBOKGUNG PALACE

This majestic palace in the heart of Seoul, South Korea, was built in 1395 by the founder of the Joseon dynasty. Destroyed twice during the Japanese invasions, it was carefully reconstructed and is being restored. With its traditional pagoda forms and richly detailed roof work, which contrast with the high-tech city of Seoul, the palace is an escape to old Korea.

CHANGE-MAKERS AND SUPERSTARS

BRUCE LEE (1940–1973)

Born in San Francisco and raised in Hong Kong, Bruce Lee was a martial artist, philosopher, actor and film maker. He died young – at just 32 – but he still became a cultural icon and a bridge between the East and West, inspiring people to take up Chinese kung fu and other martial arts, and changing the way Asians were seen and represented in Hollywood.

HAYAO MIYAZAKI (B. 1941)

Hayao Miyazaki is an influential Japanese manga artist, animator and film director. He co-founded Studio Ghibli, one of the most respected animation studios in the world. The studio has produced a host of acclaimed films, including Miyazaki's Oscar-winning *Spirited Away*.

KIM YUNA (B. 1990)

Figure skater Kim Yuna is a well-loved star in South Korea and is renowned for her elegance, musicality and technical skills. In 2010, she became the first South Korean skater to win an Olympic gold medal after a record-breaking performance. She was the first female skater to win all four major international skating competitions – the Olympics, the World Skating Championships, the Four Continents Championships, and the Grand Prix Final!

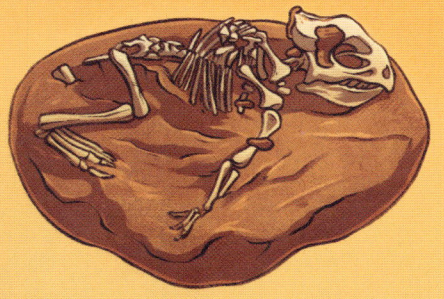

DR BOLORTSETSEG (BOLOR) MINJIN (B. 1973)

Bolor Minjin is a Mongolian palaeontologist who, together with her team, once found 67 dinosaur fossils in the Gobi Desert in just one week. She has set up a mobile dinosaur museum in Bayanzag so that local children can learn about these fascinating creatures.

WEI DONGYI (B. 1991)

Wei Dongyi, nicknamed "God Wei", is a Chinese maths prodigy. After winning two Maths Olympiads in high school, he was admitted to Peking University without having to take the notoriously difficult gaokao, considered to be one of the toughest exams in the world. At the age of 30, he took one night to solve a maths problem that had stumped a team of six PhD mathematicians for four months.

YEONMI PARK (B. 1993)

Yeonmi Park fled North Korea when she was 13 years old. She managed to escape across the Gobi Desert into Mongolia and eventually found her freedom in South Korea. Yeonmi is now a human rights activist who speaks out about the North Korean regime and continues to be a voice for oppressed people around the world.

TODAY, TOMORROW

THE KOREAN WAVE (HALLYU)

Hallyu, or the Korean wave, is the term used to describe the incredible influence Korean culture has had all around the world. It started in the 1990s when Korean TV shows (K-dramas) and cinema spread throughout Asia, but things took off in a big way across the world from the 2000s, led by a boom in K-pop music. Now, this "wave" is about so much more than K-pop. It's also about the global spread of Korean food, fashion, gaming, cinema, K-dramas and even K-beauty (Korean beauty products).

SMART CITIES

Smart cities use high-speed internet and deeply interconnected modern tech to make everything more efficient – from public health, transport, energy, water and waste-disposal systems to how people live and work and how they interact with their environment and the government.

China is home to over half the world's smart cities, from well-established cities like Beijing and SHANGHAI to newer ones such as Shenzhen, which borders Hong Kong. Beyond China, Seoul in South Korea is a bustling smart city and Japan has a number of projects underway too, including the Woven City being built at the base of Mount Fuji. Designed to be a "living laboratory" to test new tech, this city will include self-driving vehicles and solar-powered smart homes with sensor-based AI to monitor health as well as other robots to help with daily life!

CLEVER INVENTIONS

The Walkman, VHS machines and tapes, CDs, DVDs, the pocket calculator... you might have to look some of these things up but do you know what they all have in common? They're world-changing tech inventions and they were all created in Japan. The Walkman revolutionised the music industry way before Apple's iPod, while VHS transformed the film industry by bringing movies into people's homes! The list doesn't end there – other Japanese inventions include satellite navigation (sat nav), the QR code, the selfie stick and the earliest version of the 3D printer. More recently, Japan has been investing heavily in robots and AI too.

KARAOKE

Karaoke was invented in 1971 by Japanese musician Daisuke Inoue, who wanted to get the whole world singing. He didn't patent his invention so he sadly didn't make much money out of it but his concept – of singing into mics to backing music while following lyrics on a screen –became famous across the globe, a huge source of pride for its creator. It is still a big hit in Japan, where Karaoke boxes (private Karaoke rooms) are immensely popular.

ROBOTICS

Along with Japan, South Korea is one of the world's leading countries when it comes to robotics. Here, as well as industrial robots working on manufacturing, you will find self-driving robot delivery services, prison guards and urban patrollers to keep the streets safe. You might also see robots in restaurants, cooking food and serving customers. Or mini robots in schools as teaching assistants and educational aids. There are robots being tested out in all sorts of areas of life. Who knows what the future might look like!

THE MUSIC SCENE IN MONGOLIA

Since the 1990s, the urban youth of Mongolia have been building a vibrant independent music scene. The country's capital, Ulaanbaatar (known locally as UB), is home to jazz clubs, pop, folk and rock bands, and rap and hip-hop artists. Many of these stay true to their roots, blending traditional Mongolian instruments and throat-singing (khoomei) with other music styles. One band, THE HU, have done this with heavy metal. They made such an impression internationally that they were invited to perform at Coachella, one of the world's most famous music festivals, and the band was named an Artist for Peace by the United Nations Educational, Scientific and Cultural Organization (UNESCO).

SOUTH ASIA

South Asia is home to 2 billion people, a quarter of the world's population. The birthplace of Hinduism, Jainism, Buddhism and Sikhi (Sikhism), it is an incredibly diverse region with a long and rich history. Here you will find a beautiful mix of languages, cuisines, customs and religions.

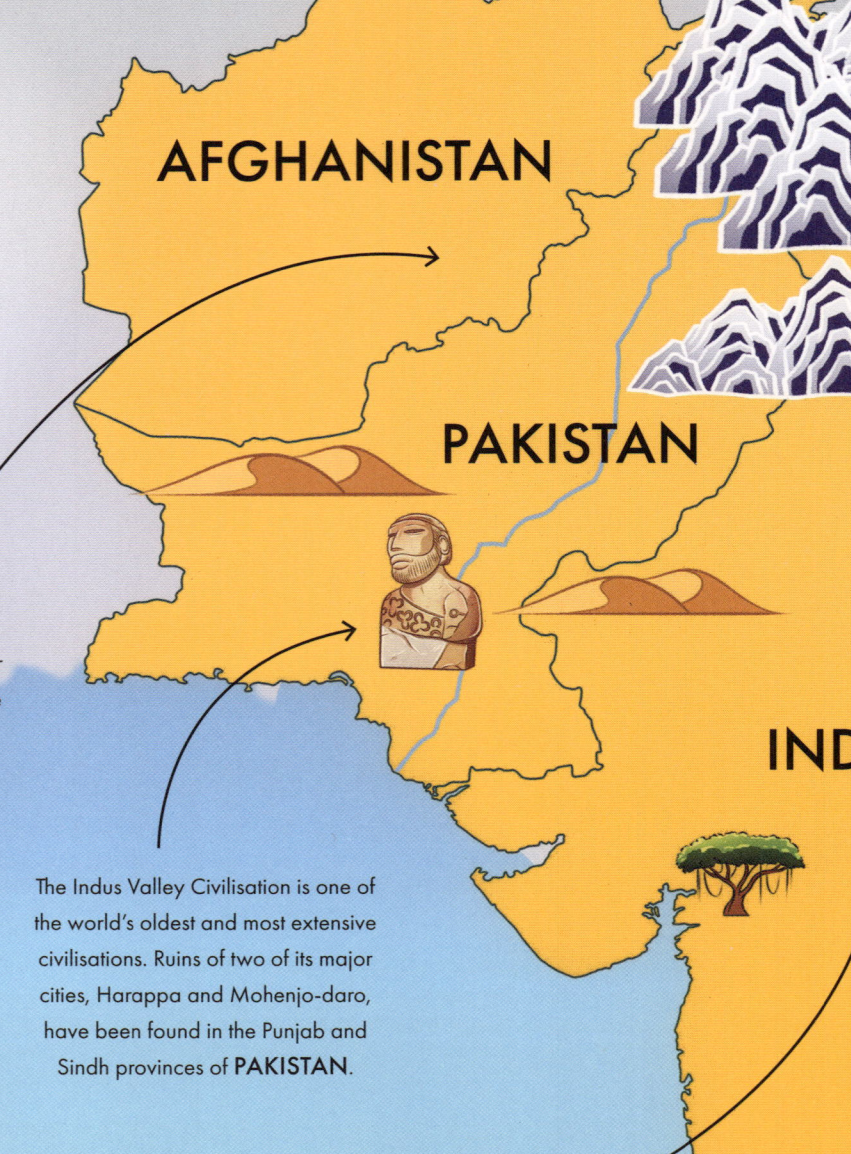

AFGHANISTAN

PAKISTAN

INDIA

Kabul, the capital of **AFGHANISTAN**, was once a city of gardens. The nature-loving emperor Babur, founder of the Mughal Empire, built the beautiful Bagh-e-Babur (Garden of Babur) here.

The Indus Valley Civilisation is one of the world's oldest and most extensive civilisations. Ruins of two of its major cities, Harappa and Mohenjo-daro, have been found in the Punjab and Sindh provinces of **PAKISTAN**.

Around 140 million years ago, **INDIA** was part of a supercontinent called Gondwana. It broke away and slowly drifted north, colliding with Eurasia 50 million years ago, creating the Himalayas.

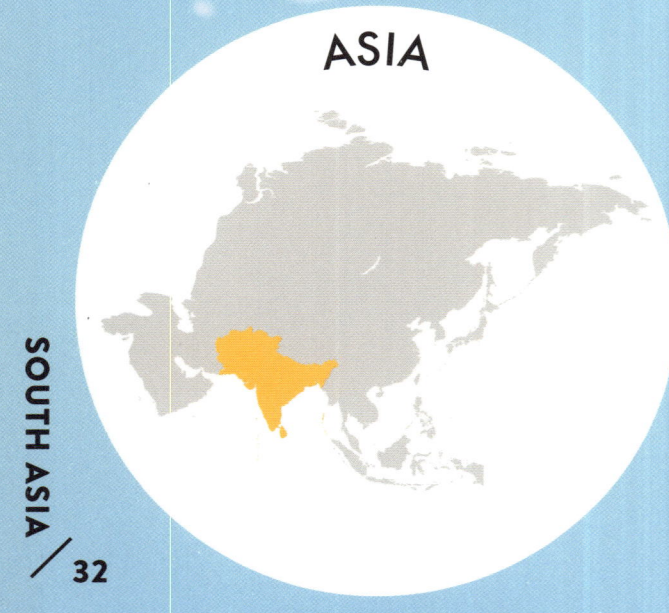

ASIA

The **MALDIVES** archipelago is made up of around 1,200 islands with bright white coralline sand beaches. But only 200 of these islands have people living on them.

MALDIVES

Eight out of ten of the world's highest mountains can be found in **NEPAL**, including Mount Everest. It is the tallest mountain on Earth above sea level and is known locally by its Nepali and Sanskrit name Sāgarmāthā.

BHUTAN is the world's first carbon-negative country. Rich forests cover 70% of its land, making it an incredible carbon sink. The government has pledged to keep at least 60% of its land under forest cover forever.

INDIA achieved independence from British rule in 1947, but the city of Puducherry (then Pondicherry) was under French rule until 1954 and the (now Indian) state of Goa was under Portuguese rule until 1961. Some of these cultural influences remain to this day.

NEPAL

BHUTAN

BANGLADESH

BANGLADESH has a rich tradition of street theatre. Plays held in public outdoor spaces have a range of themes, including important social issues.

Many fine gemstones can be found in **SRI LANKA**, from blue and yellow sapphires to rubies, alexandrite and moonstone.

SRI LANKA

THE BANGLADESH LIBERATION WAR

When the British partitioned India in 1947 (see page 35), the newly created Pakistan was divided into two parts – East (now Bangladesh) and West (now Pakistan) – separated by over 1,600 km of Indian territory. With a huge geographic and cultural gulf between east and west, tensions flared and a fierce resistance movement took shape in East Pakistan. The Liberation War began in March, 1971, after the Pakistani military launched a brutal crackdown in which an estimated 500,000 to 3 million Bengalis were killed and 10 million forced to flee the country. On 3rd December, India joined the war to support Bangladesh and its freedom fighters and on 16th December, Pakistan surrendered, a day commemorated in Bangladesh as Bijoy Dibosh – Victory Day.

A JOURNEY THROUGH TIME

2500–1700 BCE
THE INDUS VALLEY CIVILISATION

This civilisation covered over 1 million square kilometres, stretching across much of Afghanistan, Pakistan and northwest India. It had well-planned cities with sophisticated roads, water and sewerage systems and the world's first home plumbing setups. The houses had bathrooms and some even had flushable toilets!

300 BCE–1279 CE
THE CHOLA DYNASTY

This Tamil dynasty was one of the longest-ruling dynasties in the world. It originated in the valley of the Kaveri River in South India and became a major naval power. Through their military invasions and maritime trading expeditions, the Cholas greatly influenced the language, religion, art and architecture of Southeast Asia.

Shivaji

1674–1818 CE
THE MARATHAS

The Marathas were a group of clans from the Deccan Plateau who carved out a vast empire in India. They warred against the Deccan sultanates and the Mughal Empire, and managed to resist the British East India Company until 1818 when the British defeated them in the final Anglo–Maratha war.

1336–1646 CE
THE VIJAYANAGAR EMPIRE

This South Indian empire was named after its capital, Vijayanagar, the "City of Victory" (now Hampi in Karnataka). The empire was famous for its Hindu temples and palaces with elaborate stone carvings. For many years, it was a barrier protecting the Deccan and South India against the Muslim sultanates of the north.

1747–1842 CE
THE DURRANI EMPIRE

AHMAD SHAH DURRANI was a skilled military commander who ascended to the Afghan throne, united the Pashtun tribes, and established the Durrani Empire. At the time, the Durrani Empire was the second largest Muslim empire in the world after the Ottoman Empire.

1858–1947 CE
BRITISH COLONIAL RULE IN INDIA

Over the course of a century, Britain increased its control of the Indian subcontinent through the violent conquests of the British East India Company. The British government then ruled directly from 1858 to 1947, a period that came to be known as the British Raj. The wealth and resources of the Indian subcontinent, the "jewel in the crown" of the British Empire, contributed greatly to the industrialisation and prosperity of Britain and supported the war effort. Meanwhile, many millions of Indians suffered through crackdowns, massacres, poverty and famine.

4TH CENTURY BCE–11TH CENTURY CE
THE ANURĀDHAPURA KINGDOM

This ancient Sinhalese kingdom in Sri Lanka is named after its capital, Anurādhapura, which sits on the banks of the Aruvi Aru River. To grow crops in its hot, dry climate, the kingdom developed an advanced water system of canals and reservoirs.

530 BCE–1021 CE
THE GANDHĀRA CIVILISATION

The Gandhāra Civilisation rose up in what is now northwest India, Pakistan and Afghanistan and, before the arrival of Islam in the region, it was a major centre of Buddhism. Many stupas and shrines were built during this period, and huge statues of Buddha were installed in stupas and carved into rock faces.

1526–1858 CE
THE MUGHAL EMPIRE

In 1526, the Delhi Sultanate fell to an army led by Chagatai Turkic prince Babur, a descendant of Timur and of Genghis Khan. Babur's great-great-grandson Shah Jahān built the TAJ MAHAL in Agra for his favourite queen, Mumtāz Mahal. This iconic white marble mausoleum was decorated with precious and semi-precious stones including rubies, sapphires and jade.

1206–1526 CE
THE DELHI SULTANATE

The Delhi Sultanate was the first Islamic empire in India. It was established after Ghurid sultan Muhammad Ghori of Afghanistan captured Delhi. The sultanate's first and only female sultan was RAZIA SULTAN (she rejected the female title "sultana"). Her reign was cut short by her enemies but she was a wise and benevolent ruler and a formidable warrior.

1947 CE
PARTITION

For centuries, people resisted and rebelled against the British Raj. Then, in 1947, it came to an end, and British India was was divided into a newly independent Hindu-majority India and Muslim-majority Pakistan. Partition triggered a mass migration of 12–15 million people between the two countries with riots and intense violence on both sides. It is thought that as many as 2 million people lost their lives. The region around the heavily disputed border between these two countries has been unstable ever since.

2001–2021 CE
WAR IN AFGHANISTAN

In 2001, the US and its allies invaded Afghanistan to oust the Taliban regime, which was harbouring al-Qaeda, the group responsible for the 9/11 terrorist attacks in the US. The Taliban was thrown out and a new, temporary government was put in place. However, after US forces withdrew from Afghanistan in 2021, the Taliban regained control and imposed a brutally strict regime, severely restricting the rights of women.

HISTORY SPOTLIGHTS

THE GUPTA EMPIRE

The Guptas ruled over a large part of the Indian subcontinent from the 4th–6th centuries CE. This was a period of incredible innovation in art, literature and science. Elaborate sculptures were created in terracotta, stone and metals. Poets such as Kālidāsa wrote Sanskrit poems and plays. And mathematician and astronomer ARYABHATA worked on early forms of algebra and geometry, and calculated the value of Pi to four decimal places ($\pi = 3.1416$).

NALANDA

The Gupta rulers were devout Hindus but they established a Buddhist learning centre at Nalanda. It is 500 years older than the University of Bologna, Europe's oldest university. It taught medicine, mathematics and philosophy and attracted scholars from across South, Central and East Asia. It was also said to be home to a nine-storey library of handwritten PALM-LEAF MANUSCRIPTS.

Maryam-Uz-Zamani

Jahanara Begum

Nūr Jahān

THE ROYAL WOMEN OF THE MUGHAL EMPIRE

Historical accounts of the Mughal era often focus on its most famous emperors – from founder Babur to Akbar, Jahāngīr and Shah Jahān. But there were some bold and powerful royal Mughal women too. They were highly educated and often influenced politics. Wealthy in their own right, they built ships, mosques, tombs, baths, gardens and more. MARYAM-UZ-ZAMANI, for example, (also known as HARKA BAI, a Hindu Rajput princess who married emperor Akbar) ran a successful trade in silk and spices in the Red Sea. Her daughter-in-law, NŪR JAHĀN was a skilled hunter, warrior and strategist and ruled alongside her husband, emperor Jahāngīr. And as well as being a poet and running a port and trading ship, Mughal princess JAHANARA was an architect who designed and built Chandni Chowk, a famous bazaar still standing in Delhi.

Rani Lakshmi Bai

Bhagat Singh

Sarojini Naidu

FREEDOM FIGHTERS

The Indian independence movement brought together freedom fighters from across the Indian subcontinent. These men and women came from all walks of life – from royals and elite families to farmers and the working classes – and from different religious backgrounds too. Their methods of resistance and rebellion varied but they were all united by a common aim: to put an end to colonial rule. Unrest grew and grew and the independence movement kept gathering momentum over time, especially during the Second World War. Britain eventually realised that controlling these rebellions would be impossible. In 1947, the Indian Independence Act was rushed through and the British withdrew from the Indian subcontinent.

THE SIKH EMPIRE

The Sikh Empire was founded by Sikh king MAHARAJA RANJIT SINGH, who was nicknamed Sher-e-Punjab (the lion of Punjab). It was a prosperous, secular empire with its capital at Lahore. But the death of Maharaja Ranjit Singh left the empire in a weakened state and it was eventually defeated by the British East India Company.

THE WORLD WARS

Millions of soldiers who fought in both world wars came from South Asia – 1.5 million in the First World War and 2.5 million in the Second World War. Many came from villages in Punjab and Rajasthan and the hills of Garhwal and Nepal. They fought everywhere from the Western Front in Europe to West Asia, and many more toiled in factories, fields and mines at home to supply weapons, ammunition, textiles, food and other resources to help the war effort. Their contribution made a huge difference but their stories are so often forgotten.

Indian Cavalry troopers from Punjab in France, 1917.

PEOPLE AND CULTURE

TALES OF THE YETI

There haven't been any confirmed sightings but the Sherpa have many tales to share about mysterious yeti – strong, tall and hairy creatures who inhabit the Himalayas.

THE SHERPA

The Sherpa (Sharwa) are a mountain-dwelling people of Tibetan origin who live in the high-altitude Himalayan valleys of Nepal, Sikkim in India, and Tibet (an autonomous region of China). They follow a mix of Buddhism and animism and believe that the mountains are the sacred abodes of gods and goddesses, something to be revered, not conquered. Before climbing a mountain, the Sherpa make offerings of incense, flowers and food to the mountain's protective deity, asking for permission to climb and for safe passage.

THE VEDDA

This hunter-gatherer tribe lives in the thick forests of Sri Lanka. A nature-spirit-worshipping people, the Vedda are the indigenous inhabitants of the island. Traditionally, they hunted with bows and arrows, foraged for fruits, and collected wild honey. Some still live in this way but because of deforestation and urbanisation, the vast majority have had to move to villages and adopt more modern lifestyles.

THE BHIL TRIBE OF INDIA

Bhils are one of the largest and oldest tribal groups in South Asia and are found across India, from Rajasthan and Gujarat to Madhya Pradesh and Maharashtra. Historically known for their skills in archery, their name comes from the Dravidian word for bow. They wear brightly coloured fabrics and the women wear distinctive handcrafted silver and brass jewellery, including bangles, bracelets, necklaces, nose-rings, earrings, amulets and anklets.

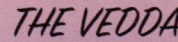

LANGAR

Langar is the communal vegetarian meal freshly prepared and served at Sikh temples called gurudwaras. It is offered free of charge to all who enter, no matter who you are, where you are from, or what your religion is. At the Golden Temple in Amritsar, India, food is cooked in giant metal bowls and hand-rolled flatbreads called roti are made on huge hot plates and in roti-making machines. The langar here serves 100,000 people a day!

THE SPICE BOX

The spice box (or masala dabba) is a staple in South Asian kitchens. Often made out of stainless steel or brass, this tin has little containers filled with colourful spices. The spice mix will vary from kitchen to kitchen but might include chilli powder, ground cumin and coriander, and turmeric as well as whole spices such as black mustard seeds, cumin seeds, cinnamon bark, cloves and cardamom seeds.

DANCE

South Asia has a rich tradition of dance. Some dances, such as bharatanatyam and kathak with their complex footwork and elegant forms originated in Hindu temples (though kathak was embraced by the Mughal courts and evolved to have a mix of Hindu and Islamic influences). Similarly, cham masked dances in Bhutan and Nepal (as well as in Tibet in East Asia) are performed by Buddhist monks in monasteries. Other dances, such as bhangra and the attan dance with their mesmerising beats on the dhol, are rooted in folk traditions. Bhangra began with the farming communities of Punjab as a way of celebrating the harvest and the open-air ATTAN DANCE OF AFGHANISTAN, banned by the Taliban, has its origins in the Pashtun tribes of Afghanistan and Pckistan.

QAWWALI

Qawwali music in South Asia dates back to the 13th century. It has Persian roots and is part of the Sufi tradition of sama – spiritual listening. It is a powerful blend of poetry and singing, accompanied by backing vocals and rhythmic clapping as well as instruments such as the tabla, dholak and harmonium. The music starts gently and builds in intensity until it reaches an emotional climax. Originally performed in Sufi shrines or dargahs, today qawwali is enjoyed everywhere from dargahs and intimate gatherings to packed concerts. This musical form, which has long been popular in India, Pakistan and Afghanistan, rose to fame internationally with the work of Nusrat Fateh Ali Khan and, more recently, through artists such as ABIDA PARVEEN.

WILDLIFE AND LANDSCAPES

In South Asia, you will come across all kinds of terrain from towering mountains and rolling green hills to mangrove forests, tropical rainforests and sweeping sandy beaches. Tigers, leopards, elephants and sloth bears roam the lands while the Bay of Bengal, the Arabian Sea and the Indian Ocean are filled with sea life, including blue whales, reef sharks, manta rays and sea turtles.

THE BENGAL TIGER

Found in India, Bangladesh, Bhutan and Nepal, Bengal tigers are fierce nocturnal hunters and the apex predators in their habitats, which means that they sit at the very top of their food chains!

THE SUNDARBANS

Cutting through northeast India and southern Bangladesh, the Sundarbans is a vast stretch of waterways, mudflats and islands in the Bay of Bengal. It is the largest mangrove forest in the world, making it a critical carbon sink. Its emerald forests and saltwater swamps are home to over 300 species of birds and a number of endangered animals from the Bengal tiger to the Indian python, the SALTWATER CROCODILE, SPOTTED DEER and Irrawaddy dolphins. Sadly, this rich ecosystem is under threat from rising sea levels, extreme weather events such as cyclones, and humans tearing down its forests for development.

THE HIMALAYAS

This majestic mountain range stretches across northeast India, passing through parts of Afghanistan, Pakistan, India, Nepal, Bhutan and China. It may be famous for its snowy peaks but it also has mountain lakes, alpine meadows and temperate grasslands, with tropical evergreen forests in its foothills.

THE SEA OF STARS

In the late summer, as night falls on VAADHOO ISLAND IN THE MALDIVES, the presence of bioluminescent plankton in the water makes the waves washing up to the shore glow a neon blue, giving the illusion of a sparkling sea of stars!

BLUE WHALES

Blue whales are the largest animals ever to have existed on Earth. Their tongue alone can weigh as much as an elephant! Once abundant, these magnificent creatures have been heavily hunted by humans and are now endangered. In South Asia, you can find them in the waters of Sri Lanka and the Maldives.

BANYAN TREES

Native to the Indian sub-continent but found across South Asia, banyan trees are fig trees with wild, wide-reaching branches and drop-down aerial roots that can make a single tree seem like an entire forest. The Great Banyan Tree near Kolkata in India covers an astonishing 14,500 square metres of land. A single tree!

BLUE MOSQUE

The original Hazrat Ali Shrine in Afghanistan was destroyed by Genghis Khan in the 13th century but was rebuilt by the Timurids in the 15th century to be even grander. Known as the Blue Mosque for its striking clay tile work and intricate geometric patterns in brilliant blues, it is an exquisite example of Islamic architecture.

SPECTACULAR SIGHTS

There are many spectacular sights in South Asia – from ancient cities and elaborately designed temples, stupas, shrines and mosques to awe-inspiring palaces and forts.

PARO TAKTSANG

Paro Taktsang is a Buddhist monastery that sits on the side of a mountain in Bhutan, 3,000 metres above the Paro valley. Built in the 17th century and reconstructed after a fire in 1998, this breathtaking complex with its white-washed walls and rooftops painted red and gold shimmers on the cliffside. The way up is long and difficult. It takes hours and hours to climb the steep mountain paths cutting through thick pine forests. On the way you will pass prayer flags with messages of peace, strength, wisdom and fortune. It is thought that when the breeze touches them, it carries their good wishes to people everywhere.

SIGIRIYA

Stretching up from the jungle and towering over the central plains of Sri Lanka, Sigiriya ("lion rock") is an ancient rock fortress. Built in the 5th century during the reign of Mauryan king Kashyapa, the stairway leading up to the fortress is carved into the rock between two enormous lion paws.

VARANASI

Also known as Banaras or Kashi, the ancient city of Varanasi with its ghats (riverfront steps), terraces and temples, lies on the western bank of the River Ganga. It is the oldest continuously inhabited city in India and, along with its river, it has a deep spiritual significance to Hindus.

CHANGE-MAKERS AND SUPERSTARS

TASNEEM ZEHRA HUSAIN (BIRTH DATE UNKNOWN)

Tasneem Zehra Husain is a theoretical physicist, specialising in string theory – an incredibly complex area of physics that explores the smallest building blocks of the universe! She is Pakistan's first female string theorist and the first woman in Pakistan to earn a PhD in string theory.

DR ASHA DE VOS (B. 1979)

Dr Asha de Vos is a Sri Lankan marine biologist and ocean educator who led the world's first long-term research project into blue whales in the Indian Ocean. She also founded Oceanswell to inspire and train the next generation of marine conservationists.

SACHIN TENDULKAR (B. 1973)

Nicknamed the Little Master, Sachin Tendulkar is a retired Indian cricketer considered to be one of the best batsmen of his time. He played his first international match at the age of 16, has scored more runs in his career than any other player, and is the only cricketer in the world to score 100 centuries (hundred-run scores) in international cricket.

ZOHRA ORCHESTRA

The Zohra Orchestra is Afghanistan's first all-women's orchestra. Once based in Kabul, the orchestra had to flee the country when music – traditionally a big part of Afghan culture – was banned by the Taliban, an extremist group that most recently took control of the country in 2021. Inspiring role models using music for social change, the orchestra now performs all over the world.

TENZING NORGAY (c.1915–1986)

Sherpa (Sharwa) Tenzing Norgay was a bold mountaineer and one of the first people to set foot on the summit of Mount Everest (Sāgarmāthā) – the other was his climbing partner, Edmund Hillary. He had attempted to scale this unforgiving peak six times but he persevered and on the seventh attempt, in 1953, he finally succeeded!

MUHAMMAD YUNUS (B. 1940)

Muhammad Yunus is a Bangladeshi economist and founder of the Grameen Bank, which provides microcredit (tiny loans) to people with very little money (mostly women) so that they can start their own businesses and support their families. In 2006, he and his bank were awarded the Nobel Peace Prize for the difference they made to the lives of millions of people.

TODAY, TOMORROW

LIGHTS, CAMERA, ACTION!

Bollywood, the Mumbai-based Indian cinema industry, is one of the largest film industries in the world. All kinds of films are made here but Bollywood is known for its glitz and glamour, its colourful costumes and scenic sets, and its vibrant music, songs and dance sequences. You'll often hear Bollywood songs blasting from rickshaws, cars, buses and trucks across South Asia. But Bollywood isn't the only movie business in the mix! There is also Lollywood in Lahore, Pakistan, with its Urdu and Punjabi films and a number of regional language movie-making hubs across India. South Indian cinema, for example, is thriving and "Naatu Naatu", a song from the Telugu film *RRR* made history in 2023 by becoming the first Indian film song to win an Oscar for Best Original Song.

Child monks playing

SEEKING HAPPINESS

In 1972, the fourth king of the Himalayan Kingdom of Bhutan, King Jigme Singye Wangchuk, declared that measuring national happiness was more important than just measuring how strong the country's economy was. Since then, and especially since the creation of its Gross National Happiness Index in 2008, Bhutan has put happiness at the heart of all its big decisions. Inspired by Buddhist philosophy, this index tracks how the country is doing based on the mental and physical wellbeing of its people, education, governance, community, culture and the environment. The system isn't perfect and Bhutan has many challenges to overcome. Still, while basing its policies on increasing happiness, the country has seen a significant increase in life expectancy as well as a reduction in extreme poverty.

STREET CRICKET

Cricket is a team-based sport that is loved across South Asia. Cricket matches draw huge crowds and hundreds of millions of TV viewers. Many of the region's well-loved stars started out playing street cricket with rubber balls or taped-up tennis balls and stumps made from things like crates, an old tyre or a pile of bricks. You'll find boys and girls of all ages playing street cricket everywhere from Colombo, Mumbai and Kathmandu to Dhaka, Karachi and Kabul as well as in villages, fields and valleys across the region. Sometimes they play after school or in the early hours to avoid the scorching sun. During the Islamic holy month of Ramadan, street matches start up after late-night prayers. Who knows – some of these young players might one day make it big!

JUGAAD

All over the world, where resources are hard to come by, people come up with creative ways to fix problems and get things done using what little is available. In India, Pakistan and Bangladesh, it's called jugaad – "frugal innovation" or a "hack". Makeshift showers and hoses are made by attaching bottles or tubs with holes in them to the water pipe. Bicycles are used to power small machines, and various parts of old and abandoned vehicles are mashed up to create new ones – half-motorbike/half-tractor, for example, or A BICYCLE FRONT CONNECTED TO A CART OR PLATFORM to squeeze in extra passengers. Now, these quick fixes aren't exactly going to fly through health and safety tests(!), but they're incredible examples of human ingenuity. They inspire the world of business too because they show just how much can be achieved with limited resources!

SOUTHEAST ASIA

Southeast Asia is a rich tapestry of cultures and scenic landscapes, and the region has a fascinating history. There is so much to discover here – from floating markets and ancient temples to dense rainforests, rivers and waterfalls.

The people of **LAOS** consume a LOT of sticky rice. They love it so much that they call themselves luk khao niaow, which means "children (or descendants) of sticky rice"!

MYANMAR

VIETNAM

LAOS

Today, there are over 3,000 Buddhist temples and stupas still standing in the ancient city of Bagan on the banks of the Irrawaddy River in MYANMAR.

THAILAND

CAMBODIA

The Thai name for Bangkok, the capital of THAILAND, is Krung Thep Maha Nakhon (roughly translating to "great city of angels"), which is actually short for the ceremonial name Krung Thep Mahanakhon Amon Rattanakosin Mahinthara Ayuthaya Mahadilok Phop Noppharat Ratchathani Burirom Udomratchaniwet Mahasathan Amon Piman Awatan Sathit Sakkathattiya Witsanukam Prasit!

MALAYSIA is a melting pot of cultures with a large Malay population but significant numbers of Chinese people, Indians and many other ethnic groups.

MALAYSIA

SINGAPORE

INDONESIA

SINGAPORE is difficult to see on this map as it's so small. It is one of only three city-states in the world. The other two are Monaco and Vatican City.

ASIA

VIETNAM is home to Son Doong, the world's largest cave. It is so big that you could fit a block of 40-storey New York City skyscrapers inside it!

THE PHILIPPINES

The PHILIPPINES' iconic "jeepneys" are colourful and affordable minibuses created out of military jeeps left behind by the US after the Second World War. They are being phased out for safer, eco-friendly alternatives but for now they can still be seen hurtling through the streets of Manila.

The Tonle Sap lake in CAMBODIA is the largest freshwater lake in Southeast Asia and is a nesting-ground for milky storks and spot-billed pelicans.

BRUNEI

Kampong Ayer, the "water village" of BRUNEI, is a cluster of vibrant villages with thousands of colourful wooden buildings on stilts.

The rainforests of INDONESIA are the third largest in the world after the Amazon and the Congo and are home to 10% of the world's known plant species.

TIMOR-LESTE

Part of the Coral Triangle, TIMOR-LESTE is a tiny country with around 400 species of reef-building coral.

A JOURNEY THROUGH TIME

2ND–17TH CENTURY CE
THE KINGDOM OF CHAMPA

The Kingdom of Champa stretched along the coast of what is now central and southern Vietnam. It was greatly influenced by ancient India and Hindu mythology. It was also a busy seaport with a vast trade network in gems, spices, silks and agarwood.

7TH–13TH CENTURY CE
THE SRIVIJAYA KINGDOM

The Srivijaya Kingdom was a powerful maritime trading empire and a "floating kingdom" based on the Indonesian island of Sumatra and extending into Java and the Malay Peninsula. Sumatra was rich in resources – including *GOLD* – and the empire, which controlled the Malacca and Sunda Straits, grew wealthy from trade in the Indian Ocean.

16TH–20TH CENTURY CE
THE ARRIVAL OF EUROPEANS

The Portuguese were the first Europeans to arrive in Southeast Asia in search of what they called the Spice Islands. It was a quest to cut out Arab and Venetian traders, who controlled the lucrative spice trade and kept the location of these islands a secret. The Spanish and Dutch followed, and later so did the British and the French. Over the centuries, these European powers colonised almost all of Southeast Asia.

1531–1752 CE
THE TOUNGOO DYNASTY

The Toungoo Dynasty of Burma (Myanmar) once ruled over what was, for a time, the largest empire in mainland Southeast Asia. It reached its peak under King Bayinnaung, a skilled military leader and a patron of Buddhism. He is considered one of the greatest kings of Burma.

1941–1945 CE
JAPANESE INVASIONS DURING THE SECOND WORLD WAR

During the Second World War, Japan launched a brutal series of invasions in Southeast Asia – from the Philippines, Malaya and Burma to the Dutch East Indies (Indonesia), Singapore and beyond. Japan promised it would help set the region free from colonisers and create a "Greater East Asia Co-Prosperity Sphere" based on Asian "brotherhood" but underlying these promises was a hunt for resources and a short-lived but aggressive campaign for expansion.

1954–1975 CE
THE VIETNAM WAR

The Vietnam War was a long and bitter battle between the governments of communist North Vietnam, supported by China and the Soviet Union, and South Vietnam, supported by anti-communist countries, especially the US, which was afraid that Asian countries might fall to communism like dominoes. When the war ended in 1975, the country reunited under the communist government but at a great cost. Two million civilians are thought to have lost their lives and Vietnam and its neighbouring areas were left devastated

802–1431 CE
THE KHMER EMPIRE

At its peak, the Khmer Empire of Cambodia covered much of modern Laos, Thailand and Vietnam. The Khmer capital, Angkor, famous for the impressive Angkor Wat complex, is thought to have been home to around a million people!

1351–1767 CE
THE AYUTTHAYA KINGDOM

Ayutthaya was established as the capital of Siam (Thailand) in 1351. The city became a major cosmopolitan trading hub, and the Siamese Kingdom of Ayutthaya grew to become one of the richest kingdoms in the region.

1353–1707 CE
THE KINGDOM OF LAN XANG

The Kingdom of Lan Xang flourished in what is now Laos. Its full name was Lan Xang Hom Khao, which means "land of a million elephants and a white parasol". The parasol is a reference to royalty and the elephants to the strength and power of this mighty kingdom.

20TH–21ST CENTURY
REBELLIONS, RESISTANCE
AND DECOLONISATION

Throughout the 20th century, there were anti-colonial riots and rebellions across Southeast Asia as well as other forms of resistance. Many of these failed and colonial powers cracked down violently but the strength and resolve of the people would not be diminished. The Philippines was the first to gain independence after almost 400 years of colonial rule, first by Spain and then the US.

VIOLENCE AND PERSECUTION

Extreme violence and persecution in some parts of Southeast Asia have led to tragedy in the region. For example, the brutal Khmer Rouge regime ruled Cambodia (renamed Kampuchea at the time) from 1975 to 1979, led by Marxist dictator Pol Pot. Two million Cambodians lost their lives before the regime was overthrown by the Vietnamese army.

In Myanmar, the minority Rohingya community has been targeted by the military regime and other groups for decades. The situation escalated severely in 2017 when a huge wave of violence broke out in Rakhine State. Since the 1990s, over 1 million Rohingya have had to flee the country, more than 700,000 of them since 2017.

HISTORY SPOTLIGHTS

REBEL SISTERS

In 40 CE, sisters TRƯNG TRẮC AND TRƯNG NHỊ led a rebellion against the Han Chinese, who had first invaded what we now call Vietnam in 111 BCE. The sisters rallied people from all walks of life and assembled an army of 80,000 soldiers and 36 women generals (including their mother!). Together, they stormed the citadels and drove the Han Chinese out of Vietnam. Trưng Trắc was declared queen and ruled together with her sister until 43 CE when the Chinese army recaptured Vietnam. The sisters were defeated but their legacy remained. Temples were built to honour them and their story was a symbol of resistance during French colonial rule. Even today, these two brave warrior women are celebrated every year on the anniversary of their deaths.

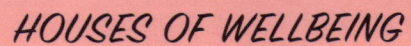

HOUSES OF WELLBEING

The Khmer Empire of Cambodia was a powerful empire and its people were incredible builders, creating temple complexes and elaborate systems of roads, bridges, reservoirs and canals. In the 12th century, Jayavarman VII, the first Buddhist king of Khmer, and his queens Jayarajadevi and Indradevi, built over 100 hospital-temples. They were called arogyashalas ("houses of wellbeing" in Sanskrit) and were home to priests, cooks and a whole team of medical workers. Outside, there were inscriptions from the king, saying that everyone was welcome there. While Europe was in the Dark Ages, in Southeast Asia the Khmer Empire had developed the world's first organised public healthcare system.

JOSÉ RIZAL AND THE FIGHT FOR FREEDOM

José Rizal was a Filipino writer, artist and physician (among other things!) who is said to have spoken 22 languages and is considered a national hero in the Philippines. He was best known for his political writings, criticising Spanish colonial rule and suggesting reforms to the rights of Filipinos. His work inspired a number of local revolutionaries. After a yellow fever epidemic broke out in Cuba in 1895, Rizal volunteered his medical skills to help the victims. In 1896, while he was on his way to Cuba, a full-blown revolution broke out in the Philippines. Though he had nothing to do with it, he was arrested and brought back to Manila where he was sentenced to death and executed by a firing squad. His legacy lives on in the Philippines where he is remembered and revered for his brilliant mind and his peaceful resistance to tyranny.

RAJA HIJAU – THE GREEN QUEEN

In 1584, RAJA HIJAU (the GREEN QUEEN) became queen of the Sultanate of Patani, an independent Muslim city-state on the eastern coast of the Malayan Peninsula. She was the first queen of Patani to rule in her own right and her ascent to the throne marked the end of twenty years of instability. She was a calm, clever and well-loved ruler who, in her 32-year reign, turned Patani into a successful trading hub and a flourishing centre of music, art and handicrafts. She was the first in a line of four formidable queens of Patani and was succeeded by her sister, Raja Biru (the Blue Queen), followed by her other sister Raja Ungu (the Violet Queen), and eventually Raja Ungu's daughter, Raja Kuning (the Yellow Queen).

PEOPLE AND CULTURE

THE HMONG PEOPLE

The Hmong belong to hill tribes across Southeast Asia. They were the very first inhabitants of the Yellow River region in ancient China but migrated to Southeast Asia from the 1700s to escape war and persecution. The Hmong are known for their colourful embroidery. Their vibrant story cloths keep a record of their history, their journeys and their legends for future generations.

THE ROHINGYA

The Rohingya have a rich tradition of music and oral storytelling. Their taranas are poetic songs that help them to express their thoughts and feelings and to preserve and pass on stories about their homeland, community and identity. These songs are often set against the bright notes of the mandolin.

BUDDHIST MONKS

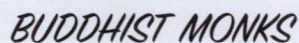

In Thailand, Buddhist monks wear robes in various shades of yellow and orange (or brown for forest-dwelling monks). They rise early – often at 4am – and start their day with long meditations, chants and prayers. In the morning, they go out into town barefoot to collect alms (offerings from local people). They have one or two meals a day (before noon) and spend the afternoon studying or teaching and doing chores before their evening meditation sessions.

Monkhood brings great respect in Thailand and is thought to bestow good fortune on monks and their families. Many Thai men become Buddhist monks for a period in their lives, sometimes for a few months or weeks, leaving the chaos of the world and all their possessions behind in a quest for calm and balance.

FLOATING MARKETS

Floating markets can be found along the waterways of Thailand, Indonesia and Vietnam and in many other parts of Southeast Asia. They have their roots in a time when there was a bustling trade along the rivers and canals of these countries. Today, if you visit one of these floating markets you can still see hundreds of wooden boats laden with colourful fruits, vegetables, flowers, sweets, snacks, handicrafts and more.

RITUAL OFFERINGS

Canang sari are little baskets of woven palm and banana leaves filled with flowers, rice and incense. A Hindu tradition in Bali, these daily offerings to the gods are a symbol of gratitude. Fresh ritual offerings are carefully put together each day and can be found everywhere – outside temples, homes and shops, on statues, in the streets, and in cars.

FOLK DANCE

The folk dances of Southeast Asia draw on the region's rich and varied cultures and history. In Borneo, for example, the MANGUNATIP DANCE (BAMBOO DANCE) of the Murut tribe is connected to indigenous healing rituals and warrior dances. The Malay dance zapin, with its Arabic beats, originated in Yemen and was brought over by Arab traders. Meanwhile, the Cambodian APSARA DANCE is rooted in Hindu mythology and the Thai MANORA DANCE-DRAMA is based on the Buddhist jātaka, tales about the past lives of the Buddha (human and animal).

Manora dance-drama

Aspara dance

Mangunatip dance

STREET FOOD

Street food is a big deal all around the world and foodies will find plenty of it in Southeast Asia – from spring rolls, sticky rice and noodle soups to fried tofu, dumplings, green papaya salads and stir-fried vegetables. Anyone with a sweet tooth will have lots to choose from too with fried bananas, sweet buns, and all kinds of cakes, pancakes, jellies, rice puddings and iced drinks on offer.

Street food is so popular with workers in Singapore and Malaysia that they have hundreds of huge food courts called hawker centres filled with vendors – a feast for the senses!

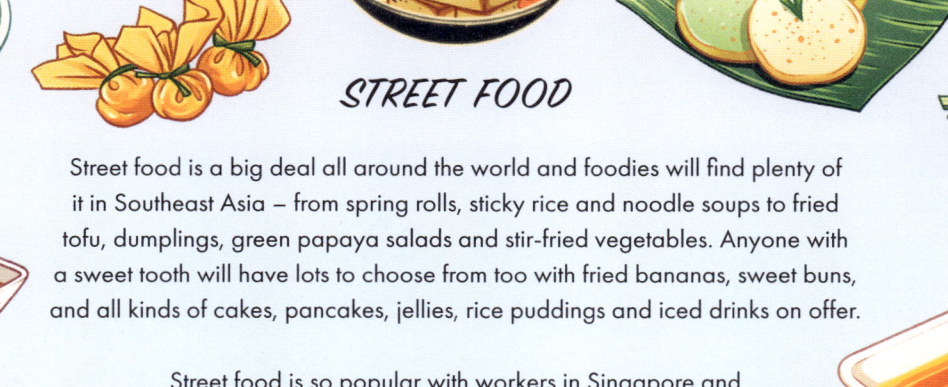

WILDLIFE AND LANDSCAPES

Southeast Asia is an incredible global hotspot for biodiversity. With its coral reefs, seagrass meadows, mangrove forests and lush tropical forests, it is home to around 20% of the world's plant and animal species. Now under threat, these beautiful landscapes and the life they support are in severe need of protection.

THE SUNDA PANGOLIN

Shy and scaly with a long, sticky tongue, the Sunda pangolin is found across Southeast Asia. To defend itself against predators, it rolls up into a ball, its thick scales forming a shield that is virtually impenetrable. But sadly, this doesn't protect the pangolin against humans who can pick it up and take it away. Classified as critically endangered, these fascinating animals are being poached to extinction.

THE CORAL TRIANGLE

The Coral Triangle is a stretch of 6 million square kilometres of ocean, including the coastal waters of Indonesia, Malaysia, the Philippines and Timor-Leste in Southeast Asia and Papua New Guinea and the Solomon Islands in the Pacific. It might not be as famous as the Great Barrier Reef but it is home to over 75% of the world's known coral species, over 2,000 species of reef fish, six of the world's seven species of sea turtle, and all kinds of other creatures from blue whales to dolphins and dugongs.

THE ASIAN TAPIR

This ancient relative of horses and rhinos has been around for over 20 million years and scientists believe it has hardly changed in appearance over that time period! The largest of all tapirs in the world, the Asian tapir is endangered and hard to find, but if you're lucky you'll see it swimming or wallowing in mud in the forests and swamps of Malaysia, Indonesia, Thailand and Myanmar.

ORANGUTANS

These gentle great apes with their shaggy red fur spend most of their time up in the trees, feasting on wild fruits, sleeping in nests made of leafy branches, and using large leaves as umbrellas to shelter from the rain. They used to be widespread across Southeast Asia but are now only found in the forests of Borneo and Sumatra. Mainly because of palm-oil plantations and illegal logging, their population has been cut in half in the last 60 years or so. Much work is needed to restore and protect these forests and save the orangutans.

THE CHOCOLATE HILLS

There are over a thousand of these unusual rolling limestone hills in the Bohol province of the Philippines. They are covered with grasses and shrubs that are bright green during the monsoon rains but turn chocolatey-brown in the dry season.

THE MEKONG RIVER

The mighty Mekong River runs through six countries in Southeast Asia, starting in the Tibetan Plateau and emptying out into the South China Sea at the Mekong Delta in Vietnam. Great civilisations have flourished in its floodplains and today it supports over 60 million people.

SPECTACULAR SIGHTS

The wonderful mix of cultures, beliefs and religions in Southeast Asia, and the love and reverence its people have for the natural world are all reflected in the beautiful cities, structures and landscapes you will find here.

HOI AN

The historic town of Hoi An with its signature golden-yellow buildings sits on the northern bank of the Thu Bồn River in Vietnam. From the 16th to the 18th centuries, it was one of the most important trading ports in Southeast Asia. Asian and European traders would meet here to hustle over spices, silks, ceramics and more, making it a melting pot of cultures. These influences can be seen today in the town's architecture from its ancient streets, clan houses and assembly halls to its tea houses, temples and pagodas – a beautiful blend of Vietnamese, Chinese, Japanese and European styles.

THE TEGALALANG RICE TERRACES

In Bali, Indonesia, lush green layers of rice paddies cascade down the hillsides. These terraces are part of a Balinese water system called subak. Over 1,000 years old, subak is based on the principle of harmony between the spirit, human and natural worlds. In this system, water flows from rivers and springs, through canals and water temples, and is shared across rice paddies.

GARDENS BY THE BAY

In the heart of downtown Singapore lies a futuristic botanical garden that is home to over a million plants from all over the world. Its 18 "Supertrees" are vertical gardens that collect rainwater and generate solar power and are home to hundreds of species of ferns, orchids and tropical vines.

ANGKOR WAT

Angkor Wat in Cambodia stretches over 400 square kilometres and is the largest religious structure in the world. Built in the 12th century, this temple city with its intricate sandstone carvings was originally dedicated to the Hindu god Vishnu and was once the capital of the Khmer Empire.

CHANGE-MAKERS AND SUPERSTARS

YIP PIN XIU (B. 1992)

Yip Pin Xiu is a record-breaking swimmer and a five-time Paralympic gold medallist. A backstroke specialist, she won Singapore's very first Paralympic gold medal at the Beijing Games in 2008. In 2022, she was the first person to receive the Singaporean President's Award for Inspiring Achievement.

CRISTINA AMARAL (B. 1993)

Cristina Amaral is the first woman pilot of Timor-Leste. She was inspired by the role of women in her country's struggle for independence from colonial powers and their stories of resistance. She decided to follow her dreams against all the odds and now encourages young girls to follow theirs too.

JIMMY CHOO (B. 1948)

Jimmy Choo is a fashion designer, famous for his made-to-order luxury shoes, worn and loved by a number of big names from Diana, Princess of Wales to Michelle Obama. He learnt the craft from his father, a shoemaker in Penang, Malaysia, and made his first pair of shoes at the age of 11!

THICH NHAT HANH (1926–2022)

Thich Nhat Hanh was a Buddhist monk, poet, author and one of the most influential Zen masters. Exiled from Vietnam in the 1960s for opposing the Vietnam War, he dedicated his life to spreading the principles of mindfulness and his message of peace across the Western world.

MINA SUSANA SETRA (BIRTH DATE UNKNOWN)

Mina Susana Setra is a Dayak environmental rights activist from Borneo who fights to protect the rights of indigenous people like her. After the land where she grew up was converted into a palm-oil plantation, she worked hard to secure a court ruling recognising the land rights of indigenous people.

MANNY PACQUIAO (B. 1978)

Manny Pacquiao is a Filipino boxing legend (and politician) who has won boxing titles in more weight divisions than any other boxer in history. Nicknamed Pac-Man, he is so adored locally that when he was a regular on the boxing circuit, the crime rate in Manila would drop right down whenever he fought because everyone was too busy watching him!

TODAY, TOMORROW

LANTERNS

Every month, on the night of the full moon, Hoi An in Vietnam comes alive with light and colour (see pages 58–59). Lanterns of all shapes and sizes adorn shop windows and line the streets and little lotus-shaped lanterns are sent floating down the river. At the YI PENG LANTERN FESTIVAL in Chiang Mai, Thailand, which traditionally marks the end of the monsoon season, thousands of paper lanterns are released into the sky as people let go of negativity and invite good fortune.

A CITY IN A GARDEN

Singapore is one of the greenest cities in the world. This is because of the government's conscious effort over the years to build this bustling metropolis into not just a garden city but a "city in a garden". In Singapore, nature is woven into the fabric of the city. Here you will find vertical gardens and green high-rise terraces, rooftops and bridges. Parks are everywhere and the plan is to make sure they're all connected – a city growing in and around a sea of nature.

THE TIGER CUBS

Indonesia, Malaysia, the Philippines, Thailand and Vietnam are known as "Tiger Cub" economies, following in the footsteps of the four fast-growing "Asian Tigers" (Hong Kong, Singapore, South Korea and Taiwan). Like the rest of the world, they have experienced some setbacks because of the global COVID-19 pandemic and climate change, but these "Tiger Cubs" have been growing steadily in recent decades. Their middle-class populations have been growing rapidly, lifting people out of poverty. These countries have been developing vibrant startup hubs as well as working on some of their biggest environmental challenges.

MUSIC SCENE

Music is pumping across Southeast Asia. Jakarta in Indonesia is home to thriving jazz clubs and cafes as well Java Jazz, one of the biggest festivals of its kind in the world. A new generation of rappers and hip-hop stars is emerging across Southeast Asia too. Often bilingual or trilingual, many rap and sing in a mix of languages, bridging cultures.

Meanwhile, P-pop or Pinoy pop is on the rise in the Philippines. The music of P-pop group ALAMAT, for example, highlights Filipino culture and colonial history as well as all kinds of social issues. The group's members come from all over the Philippines and to celebrate this diversity, their songs are a blend of Filipino languages, including Tagalog, Bicolano, Bisaya, Hiligaynon, Ilocano, Kapampangan and Waray-Waray. They want to encourage young Filipino people to feel proud of their roots.

Zamaera

Alamat

WEST ASIA

West Asia is home to the holy sites of three major world religions —
Christianity, Islam and Judaism. The region is also the cradle of
powerful civilisations that have left a legacy of art, architecture and
science. Here you will find vast deserts, oases and long coastlines as
well as bustling cities with thriving international communities.

GEORGIA is home to Vardzia, a huge cave monastery, which was fortified
by order of King Tamar in the 12th century, turning it into a wartime shelter
against the Mongol Empire. King Tamar was in fact a queen who was so
beloved and respected that she was known as a "king".

Huge carved stones discovered
at Göbekli Tepe in TÜRKIYE are,
together, considered to be the
world's first temple, dating back
more than 11,000 years.

TÜRKIYE

CYPRUS is an island divided by a long-running
land dispute between Greece and Türkiye.
Northern Cyprus is a mix of rugged mountains, a
sweeping plain and long sandy beaches.

CYPRUS

SYRIA

A collection of around
20,000 cuneiform
clay tablets have been
discovered in northern
SYRIA, dating back to
the third millennium BCE,
casting a light on everyday
life in the city-state of Ebla.

LEBANON

In the 1960s, Beirut, the capital
of LEBANON, with its hotels,
cafes, clubs and cinemas, was
a favourite spot for artists,
affluent tourists and movie stars.

JORDAN

PALESTINE

ISRAEL

West
Bank

Gaza

PALESTINE includes Gaza and
the West Bank. Olive trees have
been cultivated in Palestine for
many thousands of years. These
trees have strong roots, and the
Palestinian people consider them a
symbol of their heritage and a deep
connection to the land.

There is a
long-standing territorial
conflict between Israel
and Palestine, which
we'll say more about
on page 67.

The striking red-sand
landscape of Wadi
Rum in JORDAN is so
fascinatingly Mars-like
that it has been used in
science-fiction films like
The Martian.

A hotbed for entrepreneurship
and tech innovation, ISRAEL is
known as a "startup nation". Its
Silicon Wadi stretches across
the coastal plain and is a global
centre for technology.

ASIA

Coffee plants were brought from
Ethiopia to YEMEN, where the beans
were brewed into a drink by traders
and given the name qahwa. The
Yemeni port town of Mokha became
a big hub for the coffee trade.

There are around 400 mud volcanoes in AZERBAIJAN. These often-shallow mud cones are formed when underground gases mix with water and mineral deposits, making a gooey mud slurry that pushes up from the Earth.

ARMENIA is a nation that loves chess and has produced a number of chess grandmasters. It is the first ever country to make chess compulsory at school.

Snow-capped Mount Damavand in the Alborz Mountains of IRAN is a 1.8-million-year-old volcano and is mentioned in a number of Persian legends and poems.

GEORGIA

ARMENIA

AZERBAIJAN

IRAQ

IRAN

IRAQ is famous for the legend of the Hanging Gardens of Babylon.

Before the discovery of oil, pearl-diving was a major source of wealth in KUWAIT and in many other coastal countries such as Qatar and the United Arab Emirates.

KUWAIT

BAHRAIN is home to the Tree of Life (Shajarat-al-Hayat), a mesquite tree planted hundreds of years ago in the hot, dry desert. Miles from any large trees with no visible water source, the Tree of Life has become a local legend.

BAHRAIN

QATAR

SAUDI ARABIA is home to Makkah and Madinah, Islam's holiest cities. Each year, around 2 million Muslims from all over the world perform Hajj, a pilgrimage to Makkah.

UNITED ARAB EMIRATES

Khor Al Adaid (the Inland Sea) in QATAR is one of the only places on Earth where the soft sands of the desert meet the aquamarine waters of the sea.

SAUDI ARABIA

OMAN

The police fleet in Dubai – one of the emirates that makes up THE UNITED ARAB EMIRATES – includes a number of supercars. As well as a Bugatti and a Ferrari there are also Bentleys and Lamborghinis.

YEMEN

Once considered more precious than gold and treasured as a perfume and for its healing properties, frankincense is native to OMAN and an important part of Omani culture and heritage.

A JOURNEY THROUGH TIME

West Asia has a rich and complex history. It is here that one of the earliest known systems of writing developed, early astronomers mapped the stars and some of the world's first empires arose.

2900–2334 BCE
THE SUMERIANS

The Sumerian city-states with their mud-brick ziggurats (stepped temple towers) were some of the world's earliest complex societies. They flourished in the fertile plains between the Tigris and Euphrates rivers in Mesopotamia. Sumerians developed CUNEIFORM, one of the first writing systems, and were among the world's first astronomers!

1500–300 BCE
THE PHOENICIANS

The Phoenicians were maritime traders who lived in the Levant region along the Mediterranean coast. Skilled navigators, they created some of the most ADVANCED SHIPS of their time. They travelled far and wide to trade olives, wood, glass and fabrics, especially with their sought-after PURPLE DYE made from sea snails!

1501–1736
THE SAFAVID DYNASTY

The Safavid dynasty's empire, along with the Ottoman Empire and the Mughal Empire, was one of three major Islamic empires that rose to power in the 15th and 16th centuries. Under the rule of SHAH 'ABBĀS I, a beautiful capital was established at Esfahan, which became an important stop for traders and pilgrims.

300–100 BCE
THE NABATAEANS

The Nabataeans are best known for their stunning capital, Petra (Raqmu). They were originally Arabian nomads who settled in Jordan after building up their wealth trading frankincense and myrrh along the Incense Routes from Yemen and Oman to the Levant. Experts in desert survival, they controlled these routes for many years, growing rich from taxes.

1300–1922
THE OTTOMAN EMPIRE

The Ottoman Empire started in Anatolia and expanded into large stretches of West Asia, Eastern Europe and North Africa. It reached the height of its power under SÜLEYMAN THE LAWGIVER (known as Süleyman the Magnificent in Europe). He wasn't just a strong military leader – he was also a poet, a linguist and a big supporter of the arts.

626–539 BCE
THE NEO-BABYLONIAN EMPIRE

The ancient city of Babylon, which lies south of Baghdad in modern-day Iraq, was an important centre of mathematics and astronomy. It was also famous for its architecture, including the Esagila temple complex dedicated to Marduk, the patron god of the city, and the striking ISHTAR GATE made with glazed blue bricks and decorated with bulls and dragons.

559–330 BCE
THE ACHAEMENID EMPIRE

At its peak under Darius I, this ancient Iranian empire was the largest in the world, stretching all the way from Egypt and modern-day Türkiye to the Indus River Valley in the east with its majestic capital at PARSA (PERSEPOLIS). It was a melting pot of religions, cultures and artistic influences.

1990–PRESENT
CONFLICT IN THE REGION

West Asia has a rich history, but in recent years the region has sadly been the site of a number of wars and conflicts including the Gulf War of 1990, the US-led invasion of Iraq in 2003, and the long and tragic civil wars in Syria and Yemen. Millions of civilians have lost their lives in these conflicts, millions have been displaced from their homes, and this once vibrant and powerful region has become a place of great instability.

ISRAEL AND PALESTINE

After the First World War, the Ottoman Empire was divided up by various European powers. The British took control of the areas then known as Palestine (modern-day Israel and the Palestinian territories of the West Bank and Gaza) and Transjordan (modern-day Jordan) where, historically, Christians, Jews and Muslims had lived together peacefully. The British withdrew in 1948 following the Second World War, after making and breaking promises to various groups. As they withdrew, the State of Israel was declared, sparking the first Arab–Israeli war, which Israelis remember as the War of Independence but which Palestinians and the Arab world remember as Al Nakba, or the catastrophe. The region has been a zone of conflict ever since. More recently, in late 2023, tensions escalated dramatically with devastating consequences.

HISTORY SPOTLIGHTS

THE HOUSE OF WISDOM

The Bayt al-Hikmah, the House of Wisdom, was founded in Baghdad in the 8th century BCE. Under the rule of Abbasid caliph al-Ma'mūn, it grew from a palace library to an important centre of mathematics, astronomy, philosophy, medicine and geography. Many languages were spoken and studied in the House of Wisdom – from Arabic and Aramaic to Farsi, Hebrew, Greek and Latin. The best scholars came from far and wide to translate Greek, Roman, Persian, Chinese and Indian works into Arabic, debating and building on the ideas within them, and developing their own ideas too. It is said for every book translated, al-Ma'mūn paid some scholars the weight of the book in gold.

The remains of the House of Wisdom have never been found and some historians question whether it ever existed in this form (or at all!). But one thing is for certain – while Europe suffered through what became known as the Dark Ages, Baghdad was experiencing a golden age.

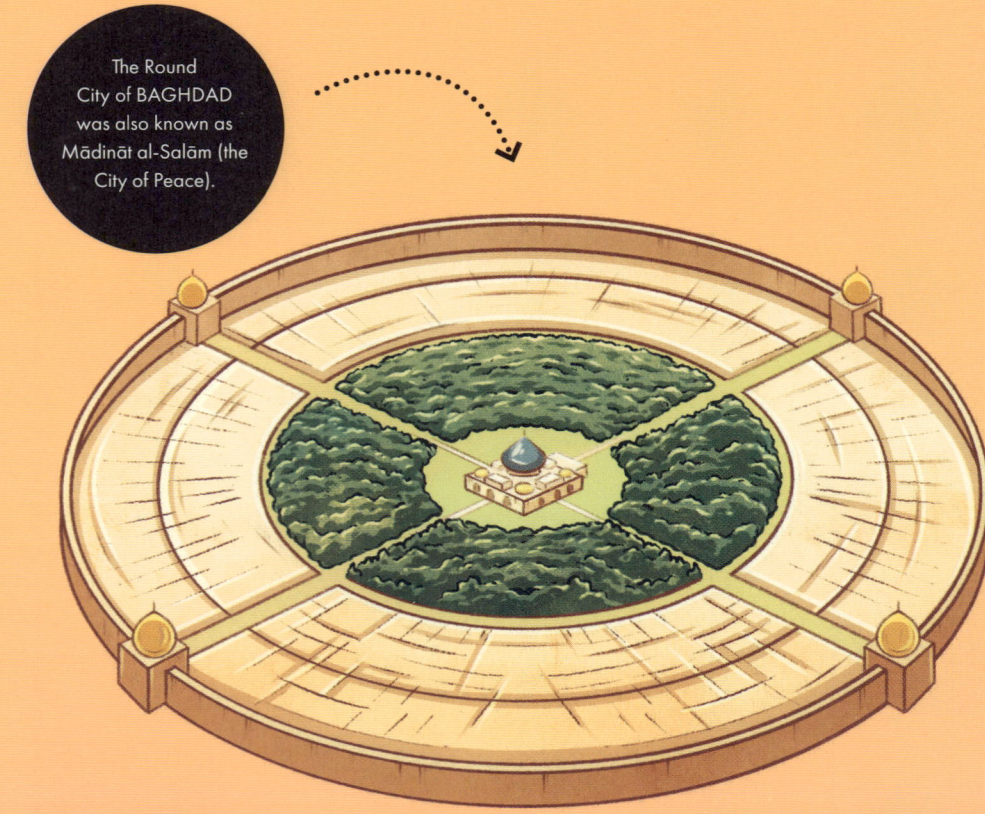

The Round City of BAGHDAD was also known as Mādināt al-Salām (the City of Peace).

ART IN THE SAFAVID DYNASTY

The Safavids are known for their contribution to the arts, especially under Shah 'Abbas I. Miniature paintings, portraits, poetry extracts and pieces of calligraphy were put together into royal albums or muraqqa, meaning "that which is patched together". Local nomadic and village textile traditions were brought into royal workshops where artisans weaved intricately designed carpets in silk and wool. Garden carpets were decorated with images of vines, flowers and forests teeming with animals – a reflection of the gardens of paradise. Meanwhile, the buildings of this era were decorated with colourful tiles and mirror-mosaic work (āīna-kāri) that reflected rays of light, creating a dazzling effect.

THE CITY OF DAMASCUS

Damascus in modern-day Syria was founded in the 3rd millennium BCE on the banks of the Barada River and is one of the world's oldest continuously inhabited cities. Today, much of this historic city has been deeply affected by war, but it was once famous for its beauty. Visiting travellers and poets throughout the ages have written about its lush gardens and fruit orchards, watered by rivers, streams, brooks and fountains. The city has changed hands many times in its history and each ruling group has added its own elements – from temples, churches and mosques to libraries, souks and bathhouses (hammāms). This mix of influences in Damascus can still be felt today.

PROTESTS IN IRAN

Protests began across Iran in September, 2022 when 22-year-old Zhina Mahsa Amini died after being arrested by the Iranian morality police for wearing her hijab (headscarf) too loosely for them. Wearing the hijab has been compulsory for women in Iran since 1983 and there are strict rules about how it should be worn. While millions of Muslim women around the world choose to wear the hijab, here it was not a matter of personal choice. In defence of the right to choose and to protest against the government, its harsh laws, and the police's brutal treatment of protesters (especially those from minority groups), many Iranian women and schoolgirls took off their hijabs, waving them in the air and even burning them to the ground and cutting their hair in an act of defiance. Women and allies stood together courageously, calling for an end to the regime.

PEOPLE AND CULTURE

MIZRAHI JEWS

Mizrahi Jews are descended from Jews in North Africa and various parts of West Asia – from Iran, Iraq and Jordan to Lebanon, Syria and Yemen – as well as parts of Afghanistan, Bukhara (Uzbekistan) and modern-day Türkiye. While they share many rich traditions with Ashkenazi Jews, who have European ancestry, Mizrahi Jews also celebrate their own unique cultures – from the languages they speak to their cuisines, clothing and music.

THE BEDOUIN

Historically a nomadic group, the Bedouin get their name from the Arabic for "desert dwellers". They are thought to have originated in the deserts of the Arabian Peninsula and spread across North Africa and the Levant. They are famous for their hospitality – diyafa, a virtue that is part of their code of honour. If you arrive at a Bedouin tent, you will be greeted with a warm welcome and hot, freshly ground coffee flavoured with cardamom, no questions asked. In Bedouin tradition, even an enemy must be given food and shelter. Today, most have settled in towns and cities, but even settled Bedouin often preserve parts of their culture – from tenting and camel-riding to traditional sword dances at celebrations.

OUD

An important part of fragrance rituals across the Arabian peninsula, oud is derived from agarwood, which is native to the forests of South and Southeast Asia. Oils are used in perfumes, and woodchips from the heartwood are burned to infuse garments and homes with a luxurious, woody fragrance with floral and fruity notes. Pure oud is so rare and treasured that it is as expensive as gold and sometimes even more so!

MARHABA
means
"welcome" or
"hello".

مرحبا

ARABIC

Arabic is a Semitic language, closely related to Aramaic and Hebrew. It is spoken throughout the Arabian Peninsula and other areas in West Asia, as well as many other parts of the world, with over 400 million speakers globally. In its classical form, it is the language of the Qur'an, the central sacred text in Islam, and Arabic calligraphy is a stunning and revered form of Islamic art. Though there are strong regional variations in Arabic, it is still a powerful unifying force in Arab culture and one that transcends religion – it is spoken by Arab Christians, for example.

DATES

Dates were cultivated in the Fertile Crescent (a crescent-shaped region between the Nile, Tigris and Euphrates rivers) as far back as 4000 BCE. These sweet fruits are a staple food and symbol of pride across West Asia and are an important part of hospitality rituals. There are hundreds of varieties of dates (600 in Iraq alone!), each with different names and qualities.

LOKUM

Lokum, otherwise known as Turkish delight, is one of Türkiye's most popular sweets. These soft, sugar-dusted jellied treats come in all kinds of flavours – rose, lemon, orange, pomegranate, pistachio, walnut and many more. Lokum are said to have been the invention of Anatolian confectioner Hacı Bekir Effendi, who set up shop in Constantinople (now Istanbul) in 1777. Four generations on, this family-run sweet shop is still standing and is one of the oldest shops in Türkiye.

Rumi

Hafez

POETRY

Poetry is deeply embedded in West Asian culture and identity. Historically, there has always been a rich oral tradition here, cutting across languages from Arabic and Aramaic to Hebrew, Farsi and Turkish. Medieval Persian poets Rumi and Hafez, for example, are renowned worldwide and much-loved even today. Meanwhile, Jewish prayer-poems in Aramaic and Hebrew are recited and sung in synagogues, at the Shabbat table and at celebrations. Modern poets from all over West Asia continue to draw on their heritage in writing as well as through spoken-word poetry, which is performed in poetry collectives, at poetry slams and even in popular TV competitions!

WILDLIFE AND LANDSCAPES

When you think of West Asia you might picture vast swathes of silent, empty desert but this landscape is rich with life (though much of it is sadly under threat). Here you will find Arabian camels and leopards, sand cats, Syrian brown bears, mountain goats, gazelles, lizards and hundreds of species of birds. Even the floor of the Dead Sea is teeming with tiny marine microbes!

THE DEAD SEA

The Dead Sea is a landlocked salt lake in Southwest Asia with a salt concentration of over 30% (nearly 10 times saltier than the ocean). At around 430 metres below sea level, it is the lowest point on land on the surface of the Earth. Rich in magnesium, potassium and other minerals, the waters and mud of the Dead Sea have long been famed for their healing properties.

Float away your troubles

You won't need your inflatable pool rings in the Dead Sea – the saltiness of its water makes it so dense that you will float!

THE ARABIAN CAMEL

The Arabian camel is perfectly adapted to the hot, dry deserts. It has broad, padded feet, bushy brows, long eyelashes and closable nostrils to keep out the sand, and a single hump that can store up to 36 kilogrammes of fat as fuel. Yes, that's right – fat, not water!

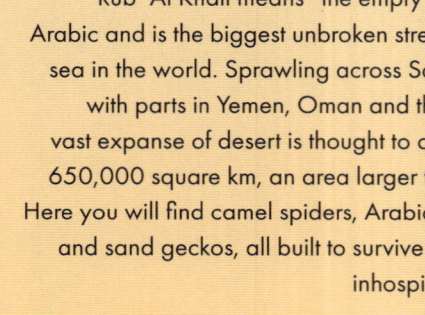

THE RUB' AL KHALI

Rub' Al Khali means "the empty quarter" in Arabic and is the biggest unbroken stretch of sand sea in the world. Sprawling across Saudi Arabia with parts in Yemen, Oman and the UAE, this vast expanse of desert is thought to cover almost 650,000 square km, an area larger than France. Here you will find camel spiders, Arabian scorpions and sand geckos, all built to survive in this harsh, inhospitable terrain.

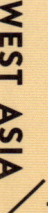

THE DRAGON'S BLOOD TREE

The Dragon's Blood Tree is named after its deep, blood-like sap. It is native to Yemen's Socotra archipelago, which lies in the Indian Ocean between Yemen and Somalia. It is an evergreen tree with thick leaves and branches forming a large canopy to capture moisture and slow down evaporation. It provides food and shelter for at least 12 of Socotra's reptile species, including various types of gecko. Once widespread, this ancient tree is now under threat from climate change, overgrazing and human development, but conservationists are working hard to reverse its decline and save this unique species.

THE CARACAL

The caracal is a wild cat with super-sensitive, pointy, tufted ears that is found across West Asia. A fierce predator, it has fur-cushioned feet that allow it to stalk its prey in near silence and strong hind legs that enable it to leap up to 3 metres high and catch birds in mid-air!

LOGGERHEAD TURTLES

Every year from May to August, hundreds of thousands of loggerhead turtles lay their eggs on the beaches of southern Türkiye. The eggs hatch two months later and the baby turtles crawl into the sea, using the reflection of moonlight and starlight on the water to find their way.

One day, some of these turtles will use the Earth's magnetic field as a navigation system to return to the place where they were born and lay their own eggs.

SPECTACULAR SIGHTS

With its unique position on the Silk Roads, West Asia is home to breathtakingly beautiful buildings and structures with a range of influences as well as refreshing natural oases offering refuge from the heat of the desert.

PETRA (RAQMU)

Surrounded by rugged mountains and deep canyons, the ancient city of Petra in modern-day Jordan was the capital of the Nabataean Empire and known to the Nabataeans as Raqmu. At its peak in the 1st century, it was a busy, cosmopolitan trading city, filled with fountains and orchards, and tombs, temples and villas carved directly into the sandstone cliffs.

JERUSALEM

Believed to be at least 5,000 years old, Jerusalem is one of the oldest cities in the world. It is of immense significance in Christianity, Islam and Judaism and its stunning skyline is lined with churches, mosques and synagogues. This breathtaking city has been fought over by many groups throughout its history and today it is a flashpoint in the long conflict between Israel and Palestine, who have both claimed it as their capital.

WADI SHAB

Wadi is an Arabic term for valleys and riverbeds that are often dry but come alive with the rains. There are many wadis in Oman and Wadi Shab, with its rocky gorge, hidden waterfall, emerald pools and palm trees, is one of the most picturesque.

GOLESTAN PALACE

Originally built during Iran's Safavid era, this palace complex in the centre of Tehran was rebuilt and extended by the Qajar dynasty from 1794. Intricately designed and elaborately decorated, it is a beautiful blend of Persian art and architecture with European influences.

CHANGE-MAKERS AND SUPERSTARS

TAWAKKOL ABDEL-SALAM KARMAN (B. 1979)

Tawakkol Karman is a human rights activist, journalist and politician who played a key role in the 2011 pro-democracy uprising in Yemen. Known by Yemenis as "mother of the revolution" and "lady of the Arab Spring", she became in 2011 the first Arab woman and the second ever Muslim woman to win a Nobel Peace Prize, which recognised her work in the non-violent struggle against authoritarianism.

TAHA BAQIR (1912–1984)

Taha Baqir was a renowned Iraqi archaeologist, historian and linguist who excavated ancient Babylonian and Sumerian sites, deciphered various Mesopotamian clay tablets and translated the Epic of Gilgamesh from Akkadian to Arabic.

QUEEN RANIA AL ABDULLAH (B. 1970)

Championing a number of humanitarian causes from education and health to the rights of women and children, Queen Rania of Jordan is a powerful voice in the Arab world. She is also a long-time advocate for the rights of refugees around the world.

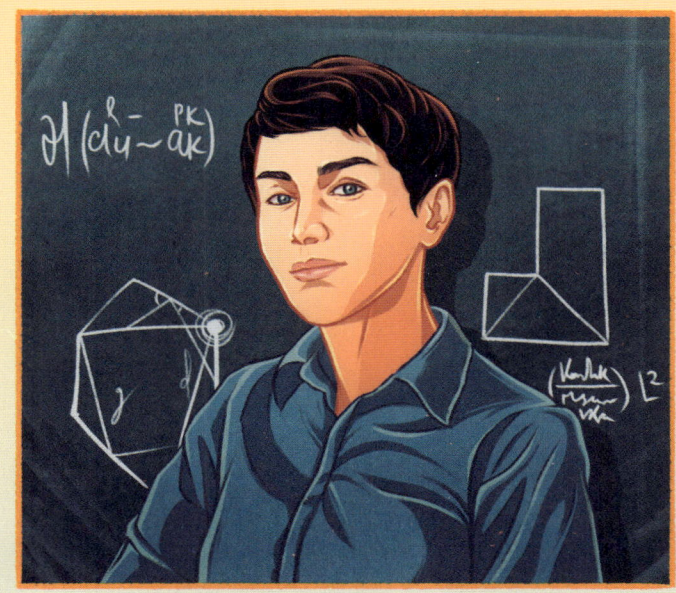

OMAR SOULEYMAN (B. 1966)

Omar Souleyman started his career as a wedding singer in Syria and grew to become an international phenomenon. His music is based on the Levantine Arab folk dance dabke with a twist of electronica. He has performed at Glastonbury Festival and the Nobel Peace Prize concert and collaborated with Icelandic superstar Björk.

PROFESSOR MARYAM MIRZAKHANI (1977-2017)

Professor Maryam Mirzakhani originally dreamed of being a writer but fell in love with mathematics. In 2014, she broke barriers to be the first woman and the first Iranian to win the prestigious Fields Medal, often described as the "Nobel Prize for mathematics".

YOTAM OTTOLENGHI
AND SAMI TAMIMI (B. 1968)

Best-selling authors, restauranteurs and renowned chefs Yotam Ottolenghi and Sami Tamimi were born in the same year in West and East Jerusalem respectively. They met, by chance, in 1999 in a London cafe and became friends and business partners. Their cookbook *Jerusalem* is a celebration of the cuisine of Jerusalem and the wider region. Meanwhile, Sami Tamimi's cookbook with Tara Wigley, *Falastin*, is a love letter to Palestine.

TODAY, TOMORROW

FALCONRY

Falconry is the practice of raising, training and hunting with falcons, the fastest birds in existence (a diving peregrine falcon can reach speeds of over 300 km per hour!). This sport has ancient origins around the world and is thought to date back to at least 2000 BCE in Mesopotamia. Today, falcons are everywhere in Arab culture. Cherished by nomadic Bedouin and an important part of Bedouin tradition, they are the national birds of Saudi Arabia, Oman, Qatar, the UAE and Yemen – and now a status symbol for the super-rich. To combat a terrible black market in falcons, these precious birds are given passports in the UAE and on some airlines such as Emirates and Etihad. They can even travel in the passenger cabin of the plane.

STARTUP SCENE

There is a growing startup scene across West Asia, particularly in places such as Tel Aviv's Silicon Wadi, DUBAI and Riyadh. As oil reserves are depleting, oil-rich Saudi Arabia and the UAE have been pouring a lot of energy and attention (and money!) into becoming thriving tech hubs. These startup-friendly hubs have a number of "incubators" to mentor and support new businesses. The hope is that some of these will one day become "unicorns" (in the startup world, these are businesses worth a billion dollars or more!).

WOMEN IN TECH AND
THE MISSION TO MARS

Women make up 60% of engineering students across the Gulf States of Bahrain, Kuwait, Oman, Qatar, Saudi Arabia and the UAE (a much higher percentage than in the US where it's 22% and the European Union where it's 26%). Women made up 80% of the science team and 34% of the mission team for the UAE's launch of AL-AMAL, THE HOPE PROBE, in 2020. The probe was designed to study the atmosphere and climate of Mars, and was the first ever West Asian mission to the Red Planet. Both the mission and the UAE Space Agency were led by a woman: Sarah bint Yousif Al-Amiri.

ART AS ACTIVISM

Art has been used as a form of protest and activism throughout the ages and across the world. Whether it's poetry, paintings, street art, stories, music, photography, theatre, film or craftwork, art can be a way of speaking out, recording events, educating people and expressing pain as well hope for a brighter future.

In Palestine, for example, the struggles and stories of the Palestinian people are captured in everything from songs of resistance and graffiti on the barrier walls of the West Bank, to the work of poets like Mahmoud Darwish and the TATREEZ EMBROIDERY passed down through generations of Palestinian women. Preserving your culture, history and identity when others wish to oppress it is, after all, a powerful form of resistance.

NORTH AND CENTRAL ASIA

North and Central Asia is a region of contrasts – from the Kazakh Steppe and the dry desert sands of Turkmenistan to the alpine forests and lakes of Kyrgyzstan and the vast Siberian Taiga.

RUSSIA is a transcontinental country, straddling Europe and Asia. Siberia and the Russian Far East form part of Asia.

The Baikonur cosmodrome in **KAZAKHSTAN** was the world's first space-launch facility. It was the launch site for both the first ever artificial satellite (Sputnik 1) and the first human space flight (Yuri Gagarin on Vostok 1).

UZBEKISTAN is double-landlocked, which is to say it's a landlocked country surrounded by landlocked countries, and it's one of only two such countries in the world! The other is Liechtenstein in Europe.

Great Vasyugan Mire

Lake Baikal

Scientists believe that modern apples have their origins in the wild apples grown in the mountains of **KAZAKHSTAN**.

KAZAKHSTAN

UZBEKISTAN

KYRGYZSTAN

TURKMENISTAN

TAJIKISTAN

Issyk-Kul Lake is known locally as the pearl of **KYRGYZSTAN**. It is the second largest mountain lake in the world (after Lake Titicaca in South America).

ASIA

The vast sands of the Karakum (Garagum) Desert stretch across around 70% of **TURKMENISTAN**. Around 30 million years ago, this area was completely covered by sea!

Over 90% of **TAJIKISTAN** is covered in mountains and hills, and it has a dense network of glacier-fed rivers and streams.

Siberia is known for its often snow-capped conifers and fierce winters but did you know it is home to the Great Vasyugan Mire, the largest swamp system in the northern hemisphere?

Siberia

The Russian Far East

Yakutsk in the **Russian Far East** is the world's coldest city. Temperatures here can drop below minus 60 degrees Celsius!

INDEPENDENT NATIONS

Five independent states were formed in North and Central Asia after the collapse of the Soviet Union in 1991: Kazakhstan, Kyrgyzstan, Tajikistan, Turkmenistan and Uzbekistan. The boundaries drawn by the Soviet Union did not take into account the ethnic and cultural make-up of the regions or how resources would be divided so these things have been a source of conflict ever since, particularly around the Fergana Valley.

A JOURNEY THROUGH TIME

North and Central Asia has historically been home to nomadic tribes who adapted to life on the steppes and in the mountains and forests. Some of these tribes joined forces to build mighty empires. In more recent history the region was shaped by the advance and eventual collapse of Soviet Russia, with five newly created nations (see pages 80–81) finding their place in the world.

3700–3100 BCE
THE BOTAI PEOPLE

The Botai people lived on the grasslands of what is now Kazakhstan. Over 300,000 animal bone fragments (almost all from horses) were found in the village of Krasnyi Yar, casting light on how the Botai herded horses, surviving on horsemeat and mares' milk.

1370–1507 CE
THE TIMURID EMPIRE

The Turkic-Mongol Timurid Empire was built by TIMUR (known as Tamerlane in the West). It was the last great empire to rise from the Central Asian steppe and at its height it stretched across much of Central Asia, West Asia, Afghanistan, and parts of Turkey, Pakistan and North India.

19TH–20TH CENTURIES CE
THE RUSSIAN ADVANCE

By the 17th century, Russia had taken over Siberia. By the end of the 20th century, it had invaded and taken over Central Asia, absorbing it into what later became the communist Soviet Union and adding 3.9 million square km to its territory.

At the time, political cartoons in newspapers often depicted Britain as a LION and Russia as a BEAR.

19TH CENTURY CE
"THE GREAT GAME"

As Russian forces advanced into Central Asia, Britain tried to use Afghanistan as a buffer zone to prevent Russia from invading India, which it considered "the jewel in the crown" of the British Empire. Afghanistan found itself at the centre of this tension between two empires in a period that became known as "The Great Game".

10TH CENTURY BCE–2ND CENTURY BCE
THE SCYTHIANS

The Scythians were a group of nomadic warrior tribes from southern Siberia who fought on horseback with bows and arrows, battle axes and spears. Many SCYTHIAN WOMEN were fierce warriors and rulers, and were buried with their weapons and horses. Some historians believe that these are the real warrior women depicted in ancient Greek accounts of the mythical Amazons.

1227–1363 CE
THE CHAGATAI KHANATE

The Chagatai Khanate covered a large part of Central Asia and was led by Genghis Khan's second son, CHAGATAI. He enforced his father's code of law so strictly that it was said that caravans on his land didn't need any guards or patrols as theft was so severely punished!

552–745 CE
THE GÖKTÜRK EMPIRE

This empire began with the Ashina tribe of the Altai, a bold people whose origin story traced their lineage back to a WOLF. Pulling together Turkic tribes from across the region, the Göktürk Empire was the first Turkic empire to dominate Central Asia, many centuries before the rise of the Ottoman Empire.

1920S–1991 CE
SOVIET RULE IN CENTRAL ASIA

From 1924 to 1936, the Soviet Union divided Central Asia into five states as part of a commonly used colonisers' strategy to "divide and rule". The idea was that these boundaries would break up ethnic groups and the people of the region would be too busy fighting each other to unite against Moscow. Not only that – under Soviet rule, the religions and cultures of the people of Central Asia were also suppressed.

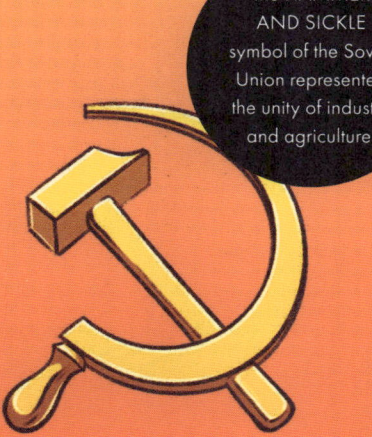

The HAMMER AND SICKLE symbol of the Soviet Union represented the unity of industry and agriculture.

1991 CE
THE COLLAPSE OF THE SOVIET UNION

When the Soviet Union collapsed in 1991, the five Central Asian nations gained their independence: Kazakhstan, Kyrgyzstan, Tajikistan, Turkmenistan and Uzbekistan. Since then, the people of this region have been reconnecting with their cultures – everything from their music and clothing to traditions passed down through the generations and secretly preserved under Soviet rule.

HISTORY SPOTLIGHTS

This is a **RECONSTRUCTION OF "DENNY"**, the mixed-heritage child whose bone fragment was found in Denisova Cave.

THE EARLY HUMANS OF SIBERIA

Deep in the foothills of the Altai Mountains, overlooking the Anui River, lies Denisova Cave, a refuge from the harsh Siberian storms. Apart from the stunning views, what makes this cave special is that it has been almost continuously inhabited by early humans and animals – including bears, hyenas and wolves – for the past 300,000 years! The remains of two early human species, Neanderthals and Denisovans, have been found together here (along with evidence of more modern humans too). When excavating the area, archaeologists even found the bone fragment of a child who was half Denisovan and half Neanderthal.

THE EPIC OF MANAS

The Epic of Manas is about the legendary Kyrgyz warrior MANAS, his son Semetey and his grandson Seytek, and is a story about bravery and the unification of warring Kyrgyz tribes. It is one of the longest poems in the world in terms of the number of lines and it is a huge part of Kyrgyz culture. Statues of Manas are found all over Kyrgyzstan and the epic has been passed down from one generation to the next by special storytellers known as manaschi. The oldest written versions of the Epic of Manas date back to as early as the 18th century, but the Kyrgyz people believe spoken versions have a much longer history.

A GOLDEN AGE OF MATHEMATICS

Central Asia, with its prime position on the Silk Roads, was a bustling centre of trade – not just in goods but in ideas. This exchange of thinking between the scholars of great civilisations between the 8th and 12th centuries led to a golden age in mathematics.

Renowned mathematician and astronomer MUHAMMAD IBN MŪSĀ AL-KHWĀRIZMĪ, for example, is considered the "father of algebra". He came from the province of Khwarazm, which is now part of modern-day Uzbekistan/ Turkmenistan, and in the 9th century he built on the ideas of Greek and Indian mathematicians and the Indian numeral system to create the foundations of algebra. In fact, the term algebra comes from "Al-Jabr" in the title of his book on the subject and the word "algorithm" comes from the Latinized version of his name – Algoritmi!

TIMUR THE CONQUEROR

Timur, the nomadic warlord and founder of the Timurid Empire, was born near Samarkand in the 14th century. He was a highly intelligent and skilled military leader who spoke Turkic, Persian and Mongolian and dreamed of rebuilding the great empire of his role model, Genghis Khan. Timur became infamous for his cruelty and his brutal campaign for expansion. Cities that rebelled or refused to surrender faced massacre, and pyramids of skulls were left on display as a warning to anyone who would dare defy his rule. It is believed that 17 million people lost their lives during his conquests.

PEOPLE AND CULTURE

THE TAJIKS

The Tajiks have Persian roots and this is reflected in their culture. The Tajik language is also closely connected to Farsi and Dari. The vast majority of Tajiks are Muslim but the pre-Islamic festival of NOWRUZ is still celebrated in Tajikistan just as it is in many countries across Central and West Asia. This Persian festival falls on the spring equinox and marks the arrival of spring and the Persian new year. In Tajikistan, the Nowruz celebrations end in a four-day public holiday, which is celebrated with bonfires, singing, folk dances, feasts, family gatherings and games.

KAZAKH CRAFTS

Traditional Kazakh crafts are deeply connected to the nomadic heritage of the Kazakh people. The scarcity of resources on the Central Asian Steppe meant that people had to create everything they needed from whatever they had available. As herders of sheep and camels, they had an abundance of wool and camel hair. So began a long and rich tradition of felting with Kazakh women making felt hats, boots and robes (chapan), as well as blankets, tapestries and carpets for their yurts, and saddle-covers for their horses.

SHASHMAQAM

Shashmaqam is a music form from Tajikistan and Uzbekistan that is thought to have originated in the cities of Bukhara and Samarkand. Traditionally sung in classical forms of Tajik and Uzbek, it brought together music and poetry (often Sufi poetry, but not always). Historically performed by both Muslims and Jews, it transcended religion and was a favourite in the royal courts of the emirs, rulers of the Timurid Empire.

BUKHARAN JEWS

Bukharan Jews settled in Central Asia along the Silk Roads over 2000 years ago. They were famous for their music and craftwork – everything from tailoring and jewellery-making to carpet-weaving – as well as their colourful kaftans with gold embroidery. They practised their religion in secret during Soviet rule and many left for Israel, the US and Europe in the 1970s and 80s, with a mass migration taking place after the collapse of the Soviet Union in 1991.

THE SHAMANS OF SIBERIA AND THE RUSSIAN FAR EAST

Shamanism is an ancient belief system. Shamans are healers and diviners or soothsayers who play an important role in the lives of the indigenous people of Siberia, the Russian Far East and parts of Central Asia. It is believed that they can use chants and ritual drums to go into trances and connect with an unseen world of spirits. They are such a big part of local culture that even people who don't follow shamanism often leave offerings for spirits, such as tea and money at PRAYER POLES, to court good fortune. These wooden poles are decorated with brightly coloured ribbons and fabrics, tied by pilgrims.

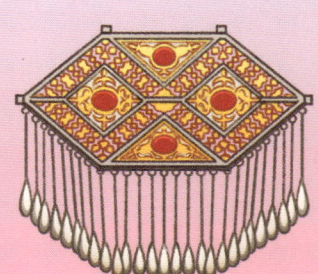

A LOVE OF BREAD

Bread is considered sacred in Uzbekistan and other parts of Central Asia and is served at every meal, often fresh from the oven. Local custom says that it should always be broken apart by hand, never cut with a knife, and should never be dropped or placed on the ground or upside down. Some iconic Central Asian breads include the soft and golden UZBEK NON and the heavier, darker-crusted Samarkand bread, both cooked in a clay oven called a tandyr.

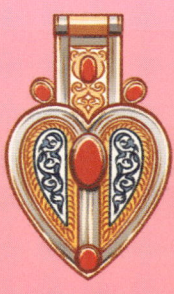

TURKMEN JEWELLERY

The silver tribal jewellery of Turkmenistan is beautifully crafted. It was traditionally decorated with symbolic images of mountains, animals, rams' horns and plants, and featured semi-precious stones, which were thought to have protective powers. The bright-red carnelian stone was a particular favourite.

WILDLIFE AND LANDSCAPES

The varied landscapes of North and Central Asia are home to a wide range of plants and animals. Some, like the Caspian seal and the nerpa, or Baikal seal, can be found nowhere else on the planet.

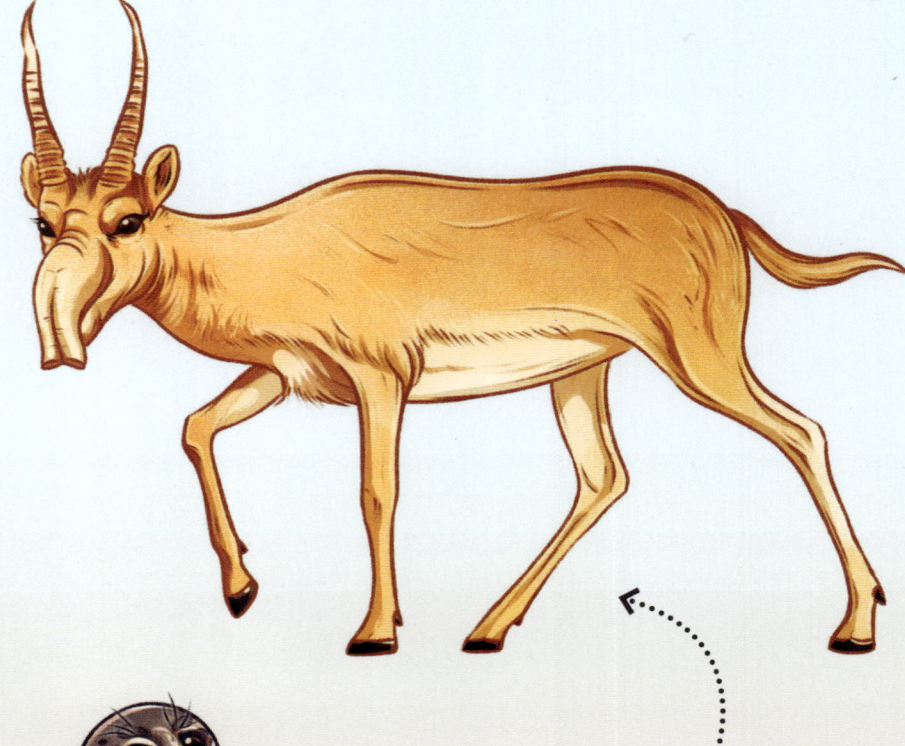

THE CASPIAN SEAL

These earless seals are found only in the landlocked Caspian Sea, which is bordered by Kazakhstan, Turkmenistan, Iran, Azerbaijan and Russia. They are some of the smallest and most endangered seals in the world. Caspian seals are hunted for their blubber and skins (and the white fur of the young pups), and their population has fallen by 90% over the last century.

SAIGA ANTELOPE

Saiga antelopes, with their distinctive floppy noses, have existed since the Ice Age! They were almost wiped out by decades of poaching, habitat loss and a deadly disease in 2015 but, thanks to conservation efforts, they have bounced back in style! Numbering fewer than 40,000 in 2005, today there are over 1.3 million saiga antelopes roaming the Kazakh Steppe.

THE KAZAKH STEPPE

The Kazakh Steppe is a vast belt of treeless grassland that sweeps across Kazakhstan and into Russia, from the Ural Mountains in the west to the foothills of the Altai Mountains in the east. Here you will find Saiga antelopes, corsac foxes, steppe pikas, and migratory birds such as Siberian cranes and steppe eagles as they stop to rest and refuel during their long journey across the world.

THE FRUIT AND NUT FORESTS OF CENTRAL ASIA

The ancient fruit and nut forests of Central Asia are home to the wild ancestors of many fruits and nuts that are loved across the world, from apples, apricots and cherries to walnuts, pistachios and almonds! Thought to have originated in the foothills of Kazakhstan, Uzbekistan, Kyrgyzstan and Turkmenistan, these fruits and nuts were carried across the Silk Roads by traders and travellers. Hybrid species developed along these routes, evolving into the fruits and nuts that we enjoy today. Sadly, these historic forests are now under threat and are in severe need of protection – 90% have disappeared in the last 60 years.

THE SIBERIAN TAIGA

The Siberian Taiga is made up of vast swathes of seemingly endless conifers – from pine trees and spruces to Siberian larch trees. Covering millions of square kilometres, it represents around a fifth of the world's total forested land and is home to Siberian brown bears, MOOSE, reindeer, grey wolves and wolverines (a type of weasel).

SPECTACULAR SIGHTS

North and Central Asia is home to some stunning sights – from crystal lakes, sunken forests and plateaus of dinosaur footprints to ancient cities that lie along the Silk Roads, connecting East Asia with West Asia, Africa and the Mediterranean.

SAMARKAND

The ancient city of Samarkand in Uzbekistan was a major stop on the Silk Roads and a halfway point connecting East Asia and the Mediterranean. Traders met here to deal in spices, silks, precious metals, horses and so much more. Destroyed and rebuilt many times, the city flourished in the 14th and 15th centuries under the Timurid Empire.

It was during this period that the magnificent Registan was built – a grand central square framed by three towering madrasahs (Islamic schools) decorated in turquoise ceramic tiles. These madrasahs and the famous Ulugh Beg Observatory were built by Ulugh Beg, Timur's grandson and a mathematician and astronomer known as the "scientist on the throne".

LAKE BAIKAL

The 25-million-year-old Lake Baikal in Siberia is the oldest and deepest freshwater lake on Earth and holds 20% of the world's unfrozen fresh water. It is home to over 1,500 animal species, many of which are found nowhere else, including the silver-grey Baikal seal (the nerpa), the only seal to live entirely in freshwater.

SUNKEN FOREST

Hidden away in the Tian Shan Mountains of Kazakhstan lies a sparkling lake with an underwater forest of ghostly spruce trees. Lake Kaindy was formed when a 1911 earthquake caused a landslide, creating a natural dam that filled with rainwater over the years. Trees uprooted in the earthquake were submerged in the lake and perfectly preserved. Just... upside down!

DINOSAUR PLATEAU

In the eastern corner of Turkmenistan, in the Köýtendag mountains, lies the dusty Dinosaur Plateau, a limestone bed containing over 2,500 tracks of fossilised dinosaur footprints! It is hard to imagine dinosaurs roaming this dry, inhospitable land but 150 million years ago, it was filled with lagoons, lakes and marshes!

CHANGE-MAKERS AND SUPERSTARS

DILSHOD NAZAROV (B. 1982)

Dilshod Nazarov is a Tajik track and field athlete who made history in 2016 when he won Tajikistan's first ever Olympic gold medal for his hammer throw. He says that at 14, he came last in his very first hammer throw competition, but his determination to get back up again and work harder set him on a path to a win at the Olympic Games.

NODIRBEK ABDUSATTOROV (B. 2004)

Nodirbek Abdusattorov is an Uzbek chess prodigy who became a FIDE chess grandmaster at the age of 13. In 2021, at the age of 17, he beat world number one Magnus Carlsen and won the World Rapid Chess Championship, becoming the youngest player ever to win the title!

BUBUSARA BEISHENALIEVA (1926–1973)

Bubusara Beishenalieva was a Kyrgyz prima ballerina. She first performed at a young age at the famous Bolshoi Theatre in Moscow, Russia. Soon, she was a star in Kyrgyzstan, touring the world and playing a number of iconic roles from Odette/Odile in *Swan Lake* and Juliet in *Romeo and Juliet* to Aurora in *Sleeping Beauty*.

DINA NURPEISOVA (1861–1955)

Dina Nurpeisova was a renowned and much-loved Kazakh musician and composer famous for playing the dombra, a traditional long-necked lute. Named the National Artist of Kazakhstan, her legacy is so important to her country that there are streets, schools, parks and even an orchestra named after her.

IZZAT KLYCHEV (1923–2006)

Izzat Klychev was one of the greatest Turkmen artists of all time. Famed for the bold use of colour in his paintings, especially his vivid reds, he was named People's Artist of Turkmenistan and, later, of the USSR (Soviet Russia). Since then, his work has been exhibited and enjoyed all over the world.

DMITRI MENDELEEV (1834–1907)

The work and discoveries of Siberian chemist Dmitri Mendeleev changed the way the world thinks about chemistry. He used to collect information about various chemical elements and note them down on cards. One day, in 1869, he organised them by atomic weight and noticed a fascinating pattern. His experiment led to the creation of the now universally known periodic table!

TODAY,
TOMORROW

Roza Baglanova

Manshuk Mametova

Olga Shishigina

Sapura Matenkyzy

Dina Nurpeisova

Kulyash Baiseitova

THE WOMEN OF KAZAKHSTAN PROJECT

The Women of Kazakhstan project is a virtual museum filled with photographs, artwork and other documents about inspiring Kazakh women from history. It was set up by Dinara Assanova to preserve and share the stories of hundreds of amazing women – from locally well-known figures, such as composer DINA NURPEISOVA and Second World War hero MANSHUK MAMETOVA, to lesser-known heroes, such as 18th-century warrior SAPURA MATENKYZY.

INSPIRING THE NEXT GENERATION

Central Asia was once an incredible centre of innovation in the sciences and mathematics. After all, this is the birthplace of legendary thinkers such as Ulugh Beg (the "scientist on the throne"), al-Khwārizmī, and Ibn Sina (known as Avicenna in Europe). In Uzbekistan, the government has been working on bringing that energy back by boosting STEAM (Science, Technology, Engineering, the Arts and Mathematics) in the region. The One Million Uzbek Coders project, for example, offers free coding courses for budding coders, while the Future Scientist competitions and "STEAM schools" aim to inspire the next generation of scientists, engineers and mathematicians.

HORSES

Horses are a hugely important part of Central Asian culture to this day. Historically, they were central to life on the steppes and along the Silk Roads, and they are the reason why nomadic tribes were able to build great empires that spanned the continent and beyond. The AKHAL-TEKE HORSES are a Turkmen breed of horse also known as Golden Horses because of their shimmering coats. Treasured for their elegance, speed and stamina, they were favoured by warriors and kings of Central and East Asia and are one of the oldest surviving breeds of horse in the world!

HORSE RACES

The At Chabysh festival in Kyrgyzstan celebrates and preserves ancient Kyrgyz horse-riding traditions. Horse races are long-distance races and the riders are often young boys who ride without saddles to lighten the horses' loads and help them go faster. A variety of horse games are played too, including wrestling on horseback!

Turkmen melon growers say that around 200 types of MELON are grown in Turkmenistan!

MELON DAY

Turkmen melons have long been famous for their sweetness – they were praised by medieval traveller and scholar Ibn Battuta as well as Babur, the founder of the Mughal Empire in India. But did you know that these melons – especially Turkmenbashi melons – are so loved in Turkmenistan that there is a holiday dedicated to them? Melon Day is celebrated every year with music, dancing, melon markets and competitions.

GLOBAL ASIA

Today, Asians live all over the world. Some were forced to move out of Asia through indentured labour or because they were refugees, displaced by war and conflict. Others moved to find work and make a future for themselves elsewhere. They have faced many challenges, but wherever they have moved and whatever the reason, they have built new lives and communities, contributing to their new homes, and making our world a richer, more vibrant place. Here are just a few examples...

EUROPE

After the Second World War and after some Asian countries gained independence, many South and Southeast Asians moved to the UK, France, the Netherlands and other European countries (and many moved earlier as scholars, sailors, soldiers and indentured labourers too). As a result, just as it has around the world, Asian culture has flourished across the continent – curries of all kinds, for example, are mainstream features on the UK food scene.

NORTH AMERICA

Asians from all over the continent have settled in North America, especially in the US and the Caribbean, where many first arrived in the 19th century as indentured labourers. Some have created pockets of culture here (and around the world!) – from Chinatowns, Koreatowns and Little Tokyos to Manilatowns, Little Saigons and Little Indias!

NORTH AMERICA

INDENTURED LABOUR

Indentured labour was a system where people were required to work for a specific period of time for very little money (or none at all). Indentured labourers often worked long hours in incredibly harsh conditions, and had to work off their indentures (debts) to earn their freedom from their "masters". The system was used to fill the huge shortfall in labour created by the abolition of slavery in the British Empire in the 1830s but in practice, it was strikingly similar to the system it sought to replace.

Millions of Asians were taken to European colonies all over the world to work on plantations, in mines and factories, and on construction projects such as the railroads. Many didn't understand what they were signing up for or were tricked into thinking their living and working conditions would be better than they were. They agreed to go in order to escape poverty and famine and support their families. Some eventually paid off their debts and returned home but others, unable to afford the journey back, were forced to start afresh in a foreign land. In this way, despite all kinds of struggles – from poverty to racism – many Asians built a new life for themselves many, many miles from home.

SOUTH AMERICA

SOUTH AMERICA

The first wave of migration from the Levant to South America was in the 19th century to escape the Ottoman Empire. Today, there is a bustling Arab community in Brazil, Peru and Chile, for example, where Arabic foods such as hummus, tabbouleh and falafel are found and enjoyed everywhere.

INTO ASIA

As well as the migration of Asians out of (and within) Asia, people from all over the world have migrated to Asia. For instance, hundreds of thousands of European Jews moved to Israel after the Second World War and the horrific persecution of Jews during the Holocaust (the Shoah). Many people have moved to Asia to seek out opportunities too, making their homes – temporary as well as permanent – in vibrant metropolises such as Singapore, Hong Kong and Dubai.

REFUGEES

Throughout history and across the world, wherever there has been unrest and conflict, people have found themselves with no other choice but to flee their homelands. Asia is no different. In the 1970s and 80s, for example, over 2 million people fled Vietnam, Laos and Cambodia for places like the US and in the last few decades, many millions have had to flee Afghanistan and Syria, with some making perilous journeys to seek refuge in Europe.

EUROPE

ASIA

AUSTRALIA

When the Australian gold rush began in the 1850s, tens of thousands of Chinese indentured labourers migrated to the country in search of the precious metal. From the 1950s, many more waves of migration from East, Southeast and South Asia have helped to turn Australia into a rich tapestry of cultures.

AFRICA

AFRICA

Half a million South Asians migrated to African countries such as Kenya, Uganda, Mauritius and South Africa in the 19th and early-20th centuries, the vast majority as indentured labourers. Some returned home while others stayed, keeping their culture alive through their languages, food and music. In 1972, however, Ugandan dictator Idi Amin expelled all South Asians from the country and seized their property. Some were taken in by other East African countries and around 40,000 refugees were taken in by the UK.

AUSTRALIA

ASIA RISING

Asia has faced many setbacks over the course of its history – from colonialism and conflict to the impact of the global COVID-19 pandemic – but it is still an immensely exciting place for so many reasons. The whole world is watching to see what the future will bring for this fascinating continent.

GROWTH AND POWER

Asia is home to the fast-growing Asian Tigers ("Asian Dragons" in Chinese and Korean!) and the Tiger Cub economies. China is a global powerhouse and India is on track to become one over the coming decades. And while the populations in countries such as Japan and South Korea are shrinking, India's is growing and the continent as a whole still accounts for around 60% of the world's population – and has a large and rapidly growing middle class with some serious spending power.

BUSINESS

Entrepreneurship is on the rise across Asia, from rural micro-entrepreneurs to startups in cities such as Beijing, Hong Kong, Singapore, Jakarta and Bangalore. West Asia has a growing startup scene too with tech hubs flourishing in places like Tel Aviv, Dubai, Abu Dhabi and Riyadh. The global Asian diaspora is also full of entrepreneurs as well as people who have made their fame and fortune in major international corporations – Alphabet Inc. (Google), Microsoft, YouTube, IBM, PepsiCo and Twitter (now X) have all had Indian-origin CEOs, for example.

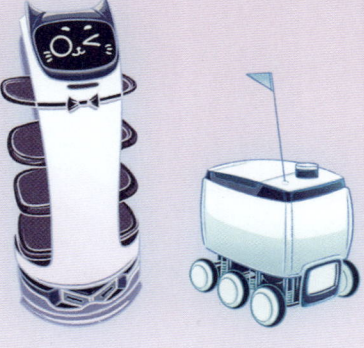

TECHNOLOGY

Asia has always been a place of innovation. In ancient times, the region oversaw the independent invention of writing, paper, printing, maps and more, as well as a number of advances in astronomy, mathematics and medicine. Today, the continent is home to more smart cities than anywhere else in the world. The field of robotics is flourishing in China, South Korea and Japan and work around AI and quantum computing is growing too. Quantum isn't without its risks but it will help solve problems even the most powerful supercomputers today struggle with – and at speed, accelerating major breakthroughs in science and technology.

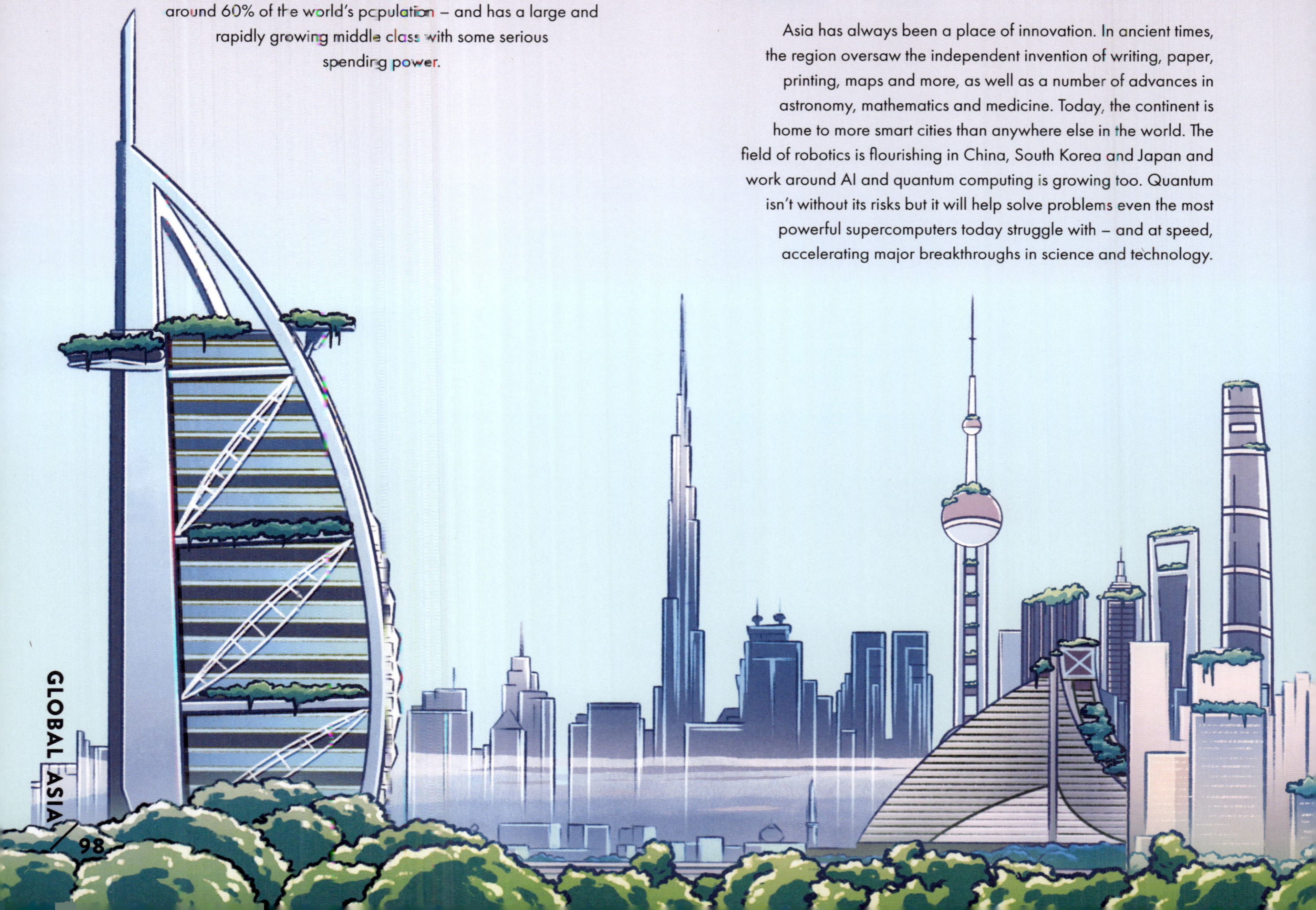

A CLEANER, GREENER FUTURE

Renewable energy is a rapidly developing space in Asia. Countries across the continent still rely heavily on coal to generate power, bringing huge challenges of carbon emissions and air pollution. However, Asia is still the world's largest market for investment in renewable energy, including solar, hydro and wind energy. There are cleantech projects everywhere as Asian countries transition to clean energy, especially in Southeast Asia. Bhutan is the world's first carbon-negative country, absorbing more carbon dioxide than it produces. Singapore is weaving clean technology and nature into its urban planning, making it one of the greenest cities in the world. And Asia's projects for the cities of the future (such as Japan's Woven City) are based on a clean, green and hopeful vision of tomorrow.

CULTURAL INFLUENCE

Asian culture and philosophy have spread across the globe through many centuries of trade, waves of migration, and more recently through TV, film, and all kinds of music from qawwali to K-pop. Hallyu, the Korean wave, is an incredible example of this but there are countless others. Ancient practices such as yoga and Asian martial arts have been embraced worldwide. Asian food in all its diversity is loved around the world and Asian fusion cuisine is on the rise. Asian fashion has long influenced global trends too. And MANGA (a form of comics/ graphic novels originating in Japan) is booming in the US and Europe. In our increasingly interconnected global society, Asia's influence has never been stronger.

CHALLENGES AHEAD

This incredible continent is full of promise but it faces many challenges – from overpopulation, inequality, poverty and pollution to issues around politics, conflicts, human rights and the environment. This includes climate change – Asia's diverse landscapes and the incredible biodiversity they support are under great threat from increasing temperatures, rising sea levels and extreme weather events. So while Asia's future is exciting, its leaders will need to make sure that growth is sustainable in every sense of the word and that everyone is brought along for the ride.

GLOBAL CHANGE-MAKERS AND SUPERSTARS

TRANG NGUYỄN (B. 1990)

Trang Nguyễn is a Vietnamese wildlife conservation scientist, environmental activist and writer. Founder of the organisation WildAct, she has dedicated her life to tackling the illegal wildlife trade in Vietnam and in the wider world through her research and her campaigns to educate and raise awareness around this important issue.

YO-YO MA (B. 1955)

Yo-Yo Ma is an acclaimed French-born Chinese-American cellist and a UN Messenger for Peace. At age seven, he performed for US President John F Kennedy. With over 120 albums and 19 Grammy Awards to his name, he plays everything from classical and Chinese music to American bluegrass and Argentinian tangos.

ANG LEE (B. 1954)

Taiwanese-American filmmaker Ang Lee is a multi-award-winning film director. A bold and astonishingly versatile talent, he makes all kinds of films, including thrillers, period dramas, superhero stories and martial arts adventures. He was the first director of Asian descent (and the first non-Caucasian) to win an Academy Award for Best Director.

DEEPIKA PADUKONE (B. 1986)

This Bollywood superstar is an entrepreneur, fashion icon, and a passionate mental health advocate. She has been named one of *TIME*'s 100 Most Influential People and has won two *TIME*100 Impact Awards for her contribution to cinema and for using her platform to raise awareness about mental health.

DAME ZAHA HADID (1950–2016)

Dame Zaha Hadid was an Iraqi-British architect and the first woman to be awarded the global Pritzker Architecture Prize. Famous for her futuristic style, her work uses sharp angles, striking curves and unusual shapes which make the strongest materials – such as concrete and steel – seem soft and flexible!

BTS

Chart-topping K-pop boy band BTS debuted in 2013 and grew to become one of the most successful groups of all time. A global phenomenon, they sing and rap in Korean and their music touches on themes of mental health and self-acceptance as well highlighting social issues.

TEN WAYS ASIA HAS INFLUENCED THE WORLD

1. PAPER

Paper as we know it was invented in ancient China around 100 CE and the idea spread out into the world along the Silk Roads. Paper money was also invented here (many centuries before the first banknotes were printed in Europe). So was toilet paper!

2. CHESS

The origins of this 1,500-year-old game can be traced back to a 6th-century strategy game called chaturanga, which spread from India, through Persia (where it was called shatranj) and into the western world.

3. MATHEMATICS

For many thousands of years, Asia has been a hotbed of mathematical innovation around things like place value, algebra and geometry. The world's first recorded use of a symbol for zero (circled in red), fundamental to modern mathematics and science, is in the ancient Indian Bakhshali manuscript, a 3rd- or 4th-century birch-bark manuscript found near Peshawar in what is now Pakistan.

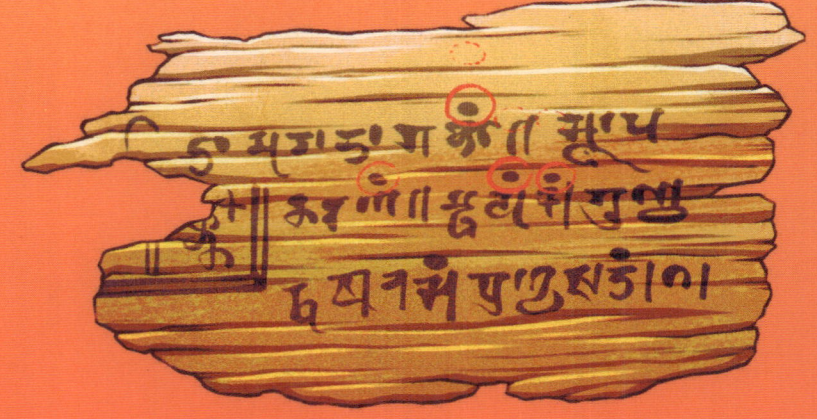

4. RELIGION

- - - - - - - - - -

Asia is the birthplace of an incredible array of
world religions and classical belief systems:
Baha'i, Buddhism, Christianity, Confucianism,
Islam, Jainism, Judaism, Hinduism, Shintō,
Sikhi, Taoism and Zoroastrianism!

5. MARTIAL ARTS

- - - - - - - - - -

From kung fu to karate, judo to Muay Thai
and tai chi, Asian martial arts are loved and
practised around the world. There are studios
and courses everywhere and countless
references in TV, film and literature.

6. FOOD

Asian food has greatly influenced global cuisine. As Asians migrated and settled across the planet, they brought their favourite flavours and recipes with them, introducing their new home countries to fragrant spices, sauces, oils, stir-fries, curries and all kinds of breads, snacks and sweets.

7. FASHION

Fashion designers around the world have been inspired by Asian styles, cuts, colour schemes, patterns and motifs as well as fabrics such as silk, cotton and cashmere. Asian fashion brands are on the rise too – from high street to haute couture!

8. YOGA AND MEDITATION

- - - - - - - - - - - - - - - - -

Yoga and meditation date back thousands of years in Asia. These ancient practices spread along the Silk Roads and took off globally from the 19th and 20th centuries. Today, people all over the world use them to find calm, reduce anxiety and improve their focus, strength and flexibility.

9. MEDICINE

- - - - - - - - - -

Born near Bukhara in what is now Uzbekistan, Persian thinker IBN SINA (known as AVICENNA in Europe) wrote cne of the most influential medical books of all time: Al Qanun F Al-Tibb (The Canon of Medicine). This vas† 11th-century encyclopaedia was translated into Latin in the 12th century and considered a key medical textbook at universities across Europe for the next 500 years!

10. GAMING

- - - - - - - - - -

So many video games and gaming systems with huge worldwide followings have their origins in Japan – from the iconic Space Invaders arcade game that laid the foundation for modern video games to PlayStation and Nintendo. Japan is also the home of some of the world's most popular gaming franchises, including Pokémon and Super Mario.

GLOSSARY

AI Artificial Intelligence or a computer or machine's ability to learn, adapt and make decisions.

ARCHIPELAGO A group of islands.

ARCHAEOLOGIST Someone who studies human history by excavating and analysing objects found in historical sites.

ATOMIC BOMB A highly powerful bomb whose explosive power comes from splitting atoms.

AUTHORITARIAN A system of government where rulers demand complete obedience.

AUTONOMOUS REGIONS OF CHINA Areas of China, such as Tibet and Inner Mongolia, with their own local governments and designated ethnic minorities.

AVIAN Relating to birds.

BCE Before the Common Era – a secular (i.e. non-religious) version of BC (Before Christ). Everything before the year 1 CE (Common Era).

BIODIVERSITY The variety of life found in an area.

CALIPH A ruler of a Muslim state.

CAUCASIAN A white-skinned person of European origin.

CAPITALISM A political and economic system where individuals and private companies rather than the central government own and control the means of production (things like land, farms, mines and factories) and operate them to make a profit.

CARBON SINK Anything that absorbs more carbon from the atmosphere than it produces (such as a forest).

CE Common Era – a secular version of AD (Anno Domini, which means "in the year of the Lord" in Latin).

CLAN A large family or group of families.

CLEAN ENERGY Energy that comes from resources (like the Sun and wind) that don't run out (or can be replenished) and which don't pollute the environment.

CLEANTECH Technology that helps reduce our environmental impact.

CLIMATE CHANGE A long-term shift in temperatures and weather conditions.

COLONIALISM A system where one nation dominates and takes control of another.

COMMUNISM A political and economic system where the central government rather than individual and private companies owns and controls the means of production (things like land, farms, mines and factories) on behalf of the public.

CONTIGUOUS LAND EMPIRE An empire whose territories are touching one another as opposed to being dotted around the world or separated by seas.

COSMOPOLITAN Describes a society that includes people from various countries and cultural backgrounds.

CULTURAL REVOLUTION The period running from 1966–1976 in China, a time of political and economic upheaval under the communist leader Mao Zedong.

CUNEIFORM An ancient system of wedge-shaped writing developed by the Sumerians in Mesopotamia.

DECOLONISATION The process by which colonised countries gain independence from colonising countries.

DEMOCRACY A political system where the people in power are elected by the people to govern on behalf of the people.

DIALECT A form of a language that is spoken in certain regions or by certain groups of people.

DIASPORA A group of people originally from one country who have spread to other countries.

DICTATORSHIP A country ruled by a dictator or dictators with absolute power and control. In such systems, all opposition is banned.

DIVIDE AND RULE In this book, refers to maintaining power or an advantage over a region by breaking up territories in such a way that they keep on fighting each other and will not unite in opposition. This strategy was commonly used by colonial powers such as the British Empire.

DYNASTY A line of leaders or rulers who all belong to the same family or ruling house.

ECONOMY A country's economy is its system of producing goods and services, and how goods and services are distributed, bought and sold within the country and traded with other countries to make money.

ECOSYSTEM A community of living organisms that live and interact with each other and their environment.

EMIRATE An area of land ruled by an emir, a Muslim ruler.

EMPIRE Where a group of nations or territories are ruled by a single nation or entity.

ENDANGERED In relation to animals, it means that there are not many left in the world and that they are at risk of extinction.

ENSLAVED PEOPLE People who have been forced to become slaves and are considered the property of another (despite the fact that freedom is a basic human right).

ETHNIC GROUP A group of people with a shared sense of identity because of factors such as their cultural background, religion, language and ancestry.

EXTREME WEATHER EVENTS Unexpectedly severe weather, including droughts, hurricanes and heatwaves.

FAMINE A hunger crisis where many people in a region have an extreme shortage of food, leading to many deaths.

FAUNA Animal life in a specific region.

FEDERATION A group of nations, regions or organisations that work together as a single unit, but keep their individual power.

FIDE Fédération Internationale des Échecs or the International Chess Federation.

FLOODPLAIN An area of flat land next to a river that often gets flooded if the river overflows.

FLORA Plant life in a specific region.

FOSSILS The ancient remains or impressions of animals and plants, often preserved in or turned into rocks.

GLACIER A large body of ice that moves slowly over the land.

GORGE A deep and narrow valley.

HAUTE COUTURE A French term used to describe the design and creation of expensive, high-quality clothes by reputable, trend-setting designers.

HOLOCAUST The persecution and murder of 6 million Jews by Nazi Germany and its allies in the Second World War. Some definitions of the Holocaust also include the millions of other persecuted and murdered people, such as disabled people and those from the Roma community.

HUMAN RIGHTS The basic rights and freedoms that belong to all human beings.

IDEOLOGY A system of ideas and beliefs that influences political systems and movements.

INDIGENOUS Originating in or native to a particular place. In relation to people, it means the original inhabitants of a land.

IMPERIAL Connected with an empire, such as the imperial dynasties of Korea.

INCENSE ROUTES An ancient network of land and sea routes where aromatics, such as frankincense, were traded.

INDUSTRIALISATION The transformation of an economy from being focused on agriculture to being focused on manufacturing.

HABITAT The natural home or environment for a plant or animal.

HOMININ A group that includes modern and extinct humans and their immediate ancestors.

HYBRID SPECIES OF FRUITS Fruits produced when two varieties of plant are cross-pollinated to create a new fruit.

K-POP Korean popular music. The K- prefix is attached to all kinds of Korean industries such as K-beauty and K-dramas.

KARST An area of land created by soft rock such as limestone, which is worn away by water, shaping the landscape.

LANDLOCKED In relation to countries, a country that is surrounded by other countries and has no coast.

LAVA Hot molten or semi-molten rock that comes out of a volcano or a crack in the Earth's surface.

LEVANTINE Relating to the Levant, the eastern Mediterranean region of West Asia. Often thought to include Syria, Lebanon, Jordan, Israel and Palestine.

LOGGING Cutting down trees to use or sell their wood or pulp.

MAGMA The molten or semi-molten rock that is formed just under the surface of the Earth.

MARINERS People who navigate or help navigate ships.

MARITIME Connected with the sea.

MASSACRE The deliberate and brutal killing of a large number of people.

MAUSOLEUM A large tomb, a special building made to house the dead bodies of a person or group of people.

METROPOLIS A large and bustling city.

MICRO-ENTREPRENEURS People who start and run very small businesses. Often used to describe small business owners in rural areas.

MIGRATION The movement of people from one place or country to another.

MUDFLATS Flat, muddy wetlands that form when mud is deposited by sea and ocean tides and by rivers.

NOMADIC Relates to the way of life of a nomad – moving from one place to another rather than having one fixed home.

PAGODAS Tiered tower structures often associated with Buddhist temples in East and Southeast Asia.

PALAEONTOLOGIST Someone who studies fossils to better understand the history of life on Earth.

PARALYMPICS A short form of the Paralympic Games, a major international sports competition for disabled athletes that exists alongside the Olympic Games.

PARLIAMENT The group of (often elected) politicians or leaders who represent the people and make the laws in a country.

PENINSULA A piece of land almost entirely surrounded by water except for one part, which is connected to the mainland.

PERSECUTION The long-term unfair and hostile treatment of an individual or group of people, often because of their religious or cultural background or political beliefs.

QUANTUM COMPUTING A new and growing field combining mathematics, physics and computer science to build computers that can solve complex problems extremely quickly.

REFUGEES People who have been forced to leave their home country to escape war, conflict, persecution or natural disasters.

RENEWABLE ENERGY Energy from sources that don't get used up (or are naturally replenished), such as wind power.

RESERVOIR A large (often artificial) lake used to store water.

RESOURCES The materials a country has and can access to increase its wealth (such as minerals, oil and fertile land).

SEMITIC LANGUAGES A family of languages that includes Aramaic, Hebrew and Arabic.

SMART CITY A city that uses advanced information and communications technology to improve how it operates.

STEPPE A vast area of dry, unforested grassland.

SULTANATE A country or territory ruled by a sultan.

SUMMIT The highest point of a mountain.

SUSTAINABLE Describes a system or activity that causes little damage to the environment so it can continue for a long time.

TAIGA A Russian term used to describe the vast (and largely coniferous) forests of North America and Eurasia.

TECTONIC PLATES Huge rocky slabs of the Earth's crust or surface whose movement can create mountains and earthquakes.

TERRAIN An area of land or type of land (e.g. rocky terrain).

TRADE The buying and selling of goods and services.

TRANSCONTINENTAL Crossing a continent. Transcontinental countries, such as Türkiye, have territory in more than one continent.

URBANISATION The transformation from a rural area into a more urban area, or the movement of people from rural areas to towns and cities.

INDEX

In loving memory of Aaji (Smt. Prashanti Sirdeshpande). Miss you so much - RS

To you, the reader, may this book inspire you to dream big
and believe in the limitless power of your imagination - JL

The illustrations were created digitally
Set in SignPainter and Futura
Maps by David Rojas Marquez

Designer: Myrto Dimitrakoulia
Editor: Nicola Edwards
Cultural accuracy checks by Charlotte al-Qadi and Eldes Tran, with Write Up.
Production Controller: Dawn Cameron
Proofreader: Kimberley Davis
Art Director: Karissa Santos
Publisher: Debbie Foy

Printed in Malaysia, CO072024

9 8 7 6 5 4 3 2 1